pitman

2000

SHORTHAND

SKILL BOOK

Bryan Coombs

Pitman Publishing

First published 1976

Pitman Publishing Ltd
Pitman House, 39 Parker Street, London, WC2B 5PB, UK

Fearon Publishers Inc
6 Davis Drive, Belmont, California 94002, USA

Pitman Publishing Pty Ltd
Pitman House, 158 Bouverie Street, Carlton, Victoria 3053, Australia

Pitman Publishing
Copp Clark Publishing
517 Wellington Street West, Toronto, M5V 1G1, Canada

Sir Isaac Pitman Ltd
Banda Street, PO Box 46038, Nairobi, Kenya, East Africa

Pitman Publishing Co SA (Pty) Ltd
Craighall Mews, Jan Smuts Avenue, Craighall Park
Johannesburg 2001, South Africa

Isaac Pitman

ISBN: 0 273 00890 0

Text set in 10/11 pt. Monotype Baskerville, printed by photolithography,
and bound in Great Britain at The Pitman Press, Bath

G6—(S.2007:26)

PREFACE

Skill Book is intended for use when *First Course* and *First Course Review* have been completed, by which time the basic phrasing principles of Pitman 2000 Shorthand will have been mastered.

Phrasing and Skill Development

A complete understanding of the phrasing principles and their use will make it possible to increase the rate of writing to sustained speeds of up to 150 words per minute. This assumes that the writer has a total command of the short forms and intersections and is producing an accurate shorthand note. The consistent application of phrasing principles promotes speed, leading to confident penmanship and the good shorthand note which is essential for rapid and accurate transcription.

The principles of phrasing in *Skill Book* have been applied to those frequently occurring word patterns which are so common in everyday use that it is seldom possible to write any continuous matter without encountering them. Phrases are not only very fast to write but are distinctive and they stand out like beacons in the shorthand notes.

The successful development of any skill takes time, effort and determination, with complete mastery coming only after consistent practice and much hard work so it is essential that some reading, dictation and drilling from *Skill Book* shall take place each day. Practising for half an hour every day ensures a buildup of confidence and speed.

Remember to 'push for speed' when reading the shorthand passages. Any outlines causing hesitancy should be checked in the key and drilled immediately until they can be recognized and read without hesitation. The passage should be read through again, aiming to read as quickly as if the matter was in typescript. When transcribing it is recommended that local addresses should be inserted in the correspondence to add realism.

Having become really familiar with the common and frequently occurring phrases in this book, the speeds required for a career in business will have been attained and it will be possible to extend the knowledge and application of phrasing in Pitman 2000 Shorthand to the special requirements of any working situation.

Acknowledgement

The author wishes to express his gratitude to the editorial staff of the publishers and particularly to Janet Job and Betty Perkins for their especial contribution to this book.

CONTENTS

v

CHAPTER 1
Tick The
Diphthongs I and U

TICK THE

Tick the should be used whenever possible because it is so much faster than writing the short form for *the*. **Tick the** is attached to the preceding stroke and is always sloped in the same direction as CH ...../..... . **Tick the** may be written upwards or downwards according to which direction gives the clearer joining:

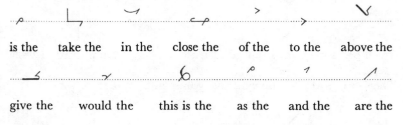

is the	take the	in the	close the	of the	to the	above the

give the	would the	this is the	as the	and the	are the

Tick the is used in the **middle** of a phrase:

in the matter	at the time	for the moment	in the course of the

The short form for *the* is used at the beginning of a sentence and after a **ST** or **STER** loop, **NS** or **NSES** circle and a half-length straight stroke standing alone and having no initial or final attachment:

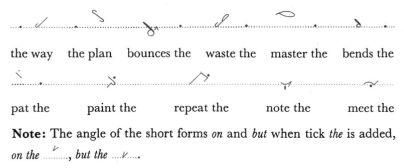

the way   the plan   bounces the   waste the   master the   bends the

pat the   paint the   repeat the   note the   meet the

Note: The angle of the short forms *on* and *but* when tick *the* is added, *on the* ...., *but the* ....

DIPHTHONGS I AND U

The short form for *I* is extensively used in phrasing:

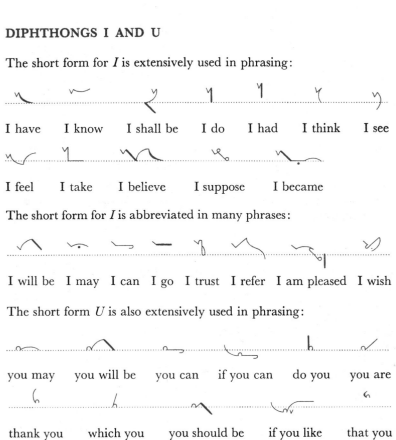

I have   I know   I shall be   I do   I had   I think   I see

I feel   I take   I believe   I suppose   I became

The short form for *I* is abbreviated in many phrases:

I will be   I may   I can   I go   I trust   I refer   I am pleased   I wish

The short form *U* is also extensively used in phrasing:

you may   you will be   you can   if you can   do you   you are

thank you   which you   you should be   if you like   that you

At the end of a phrase the diphthong **U** is turned on its side if a better joining results:

would you   are you   I agree with you   will you   let you   with you

PHRASING DRILL

(174)

CORRESPONDENCE

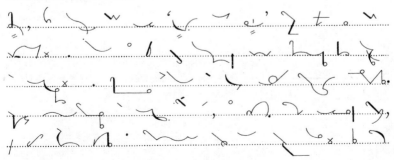

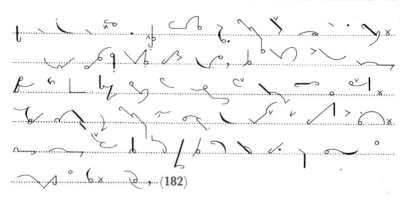

(182)

QUALIFICATIONS

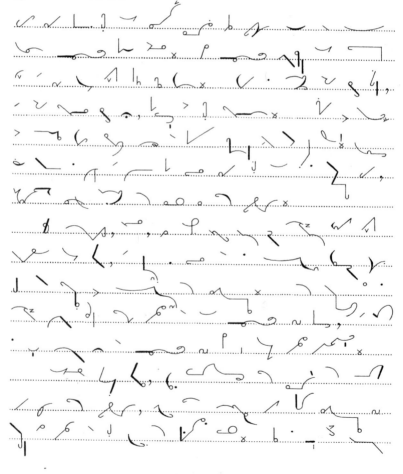

CHAPTER 2

He
Hope
Tick H

HE

The full stroke for **H** is written for **he** standing alone or at the **beginning** of a phrase:

he will   he is   he can   he knows   he said   he was

In the **middle** or at the **end** of a phrase the abbreviated form for **he** is written:

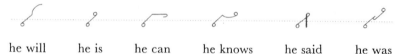

if he will   if he can   if he is/has   that he   that he will

The **H** is omitted in phrases that include the word **hope**:

we hope that you will   I hope you will   I hope you will be able to

Tick H is retained in simple joinings:

in here   for whom   for him   for her   to him   to whom

PHRASING DRILL

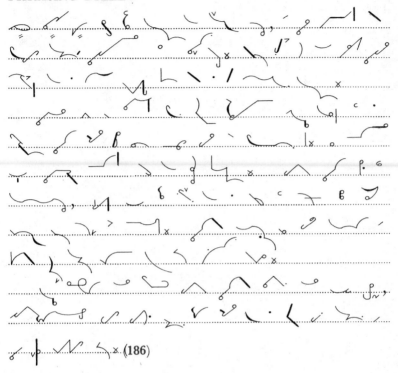

(186)

CORRESPONDENCE

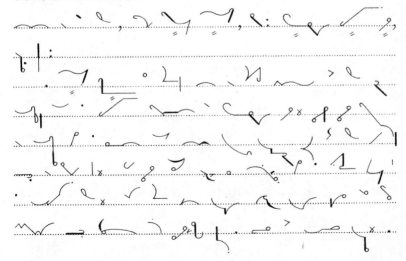

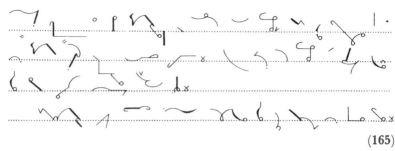

(165)

ON BEING EMPLOYED

(600)

CHAPTER 3
Circle S
Omission of a consonant

CIRCLE S

Circle S provides an excellent link in phrasing:

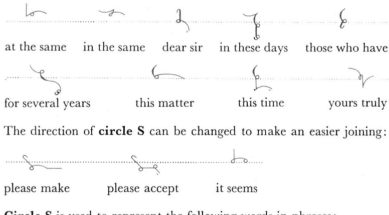

at the same   in the same   dear sir   in these days   those who have

for several years   this matter   this time   yours truly

The direction of **circle S** can be changed to make an easier joining:

please make   please accept   it seems

Circle S is used to represent the following words in phrases:

1. Is, his, as, has

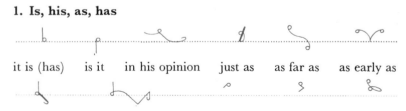

it is (has)   is it   in his opinion   just as   as far as   as early as

it has been   it is important   as (has) the   as to the   as fast as

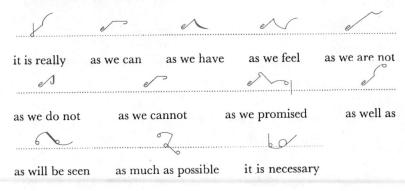

it is really	as we can	as we have	as we feel	as we are not

as we do not	as we cannot	as we promised	as well as

as will be seen	as much as possible	it is necessary

2. Us

The **stroke S** must be used for the word **us** when the outline stands alone, but **circle S** is usually written in phrases.

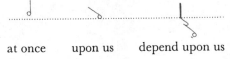

tell us	from us	inform us	with us	before us	let us	help us

3. Once, n-us

Combined with the **N hook** to straight strokes, the circle is used for the word **once** and may also be used for the word **us** following.

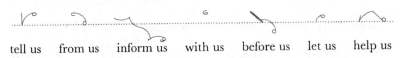

at once	upon us	depend upon us

Note: *once again*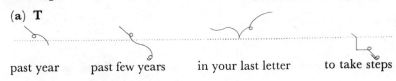

THE PRINCIPLE OF OMISSION

Phrases can be written faster and easier by sometimes omitting a repeated consonant:

1. The omission of a consonant

A useful group of phrases is formed by writing a **Circle S** instead of a **ST loop**:

(a) T

past year	past few years	in your last letter	to take steps

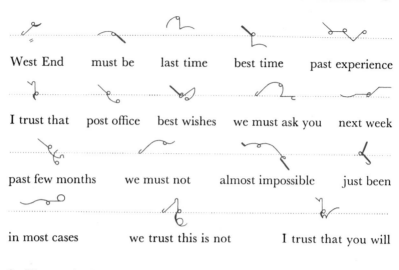

West End   must be   last time   best time   past experience

I trust that   post office   best wishes   we must ask you   next week

past few months   we must not   almost impossible   just been

in most cases   we trust this is not   I trust that you will

2. The omission of repeated consonants

When a consonant is repeated it is easier to write one consonant instead of the two repeated ones:

(a) K

take exception   take cover

(b) L

animal life   family life   political life

(c) M

some measure   Prime Minister

(d) R

satisfactory results   satisfactory records   better results   poor results

Fact

The word **fact** may be represented in a phrase by writing a half-length

stroke **K:**

in fact

PHRASING DRILL (a)

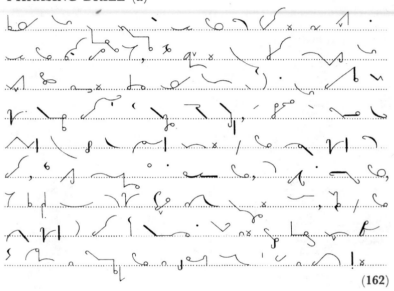

(162)

PHRASING DRILL (b)

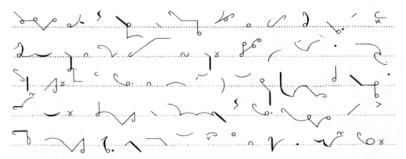

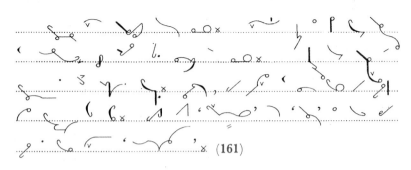

(161)

CORRESPONDENCE

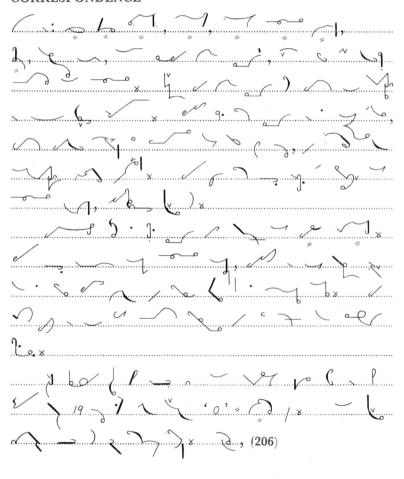

(206)

FLYING TODAY

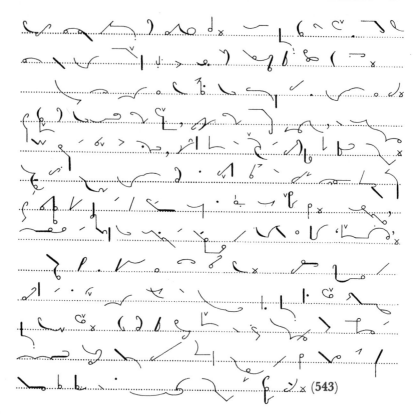

(543)

CHAPTER 4
Ses circle
Omission of a hook

SES CIRCLE

The **SES circle** is used in phrasing as follows:

1. As-s

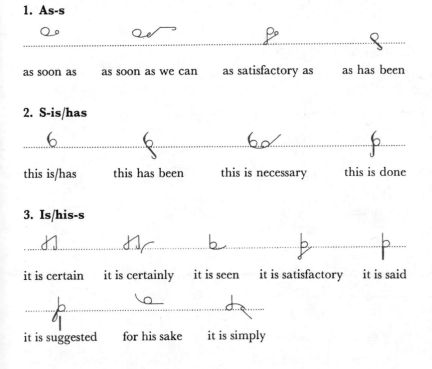

| as soon as | as soon as we can | as satisfactory as | as has been |

2. S-is/has

| this is/has | this has been | this is necessary | this is done |

3. Is/his-s

| it is certain | it is certainly | it is seen | it is satisfactory | it is said |

| it is suggested | for his sake | it is simply |

4. S-s

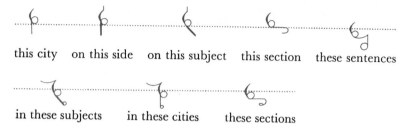

this city   on this side   on this subject   this section   these sentences

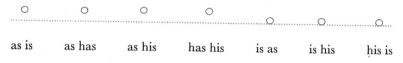

in these subjects   in these cities   these sections

5. The **Ses circle** is also used in phrases standing alone:

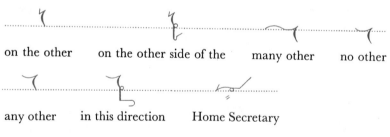

as is   as has   as his   has his   is as   is his   his is

OMISSION OF A HOOK

By omitting **R hook** and **N hook,** phrases are written quickly and are easy to read:

1. R hook

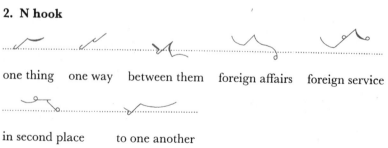

on the other   on the other side of the   many other   no other

any other   in this direction   Home Secretary

2. N hook

one thing   one way   between them   foreign affairs   foreign service

in second place   to one another

PHRASING DRILL

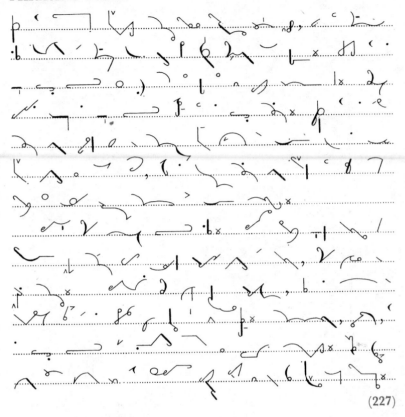

(227)

CORRESPONDENCE

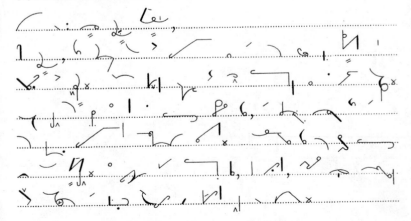

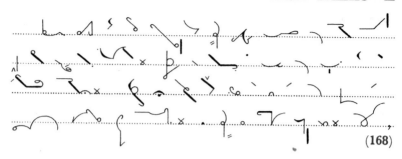

(168)

ANTIQUES

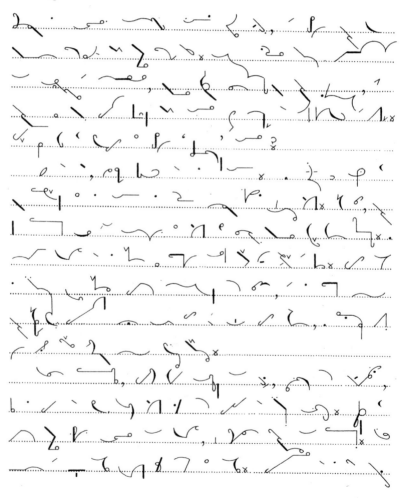

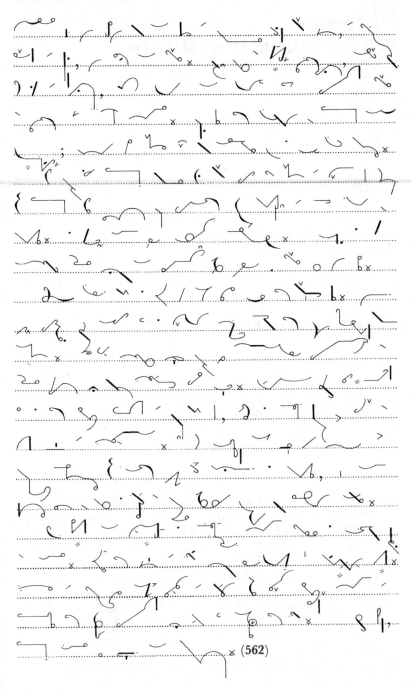

(562)

CHAPTER 5
St loop
Omission of a syllable

ST LOOP

The **ST loop** is used **medially** in phrases as follows:

| last year | last few years | last few days | just now |

Circle S follows the **ST** loop to represent **as** or **us**:

| as fast as | against us | just as |

When *first* occurs at the **beginning** or in the **middle** of a phrase, the short form is retained, but when occurring at the end of a phrase the word is represented by a **ST** loop attached to the stroke in the normal way:

| first class | first time | first thing | first instance | first prize |

| at first | very first | at first appearance | at first cost |

OMISSION OF A SYLLABLE

By omitting a syllable, phrases are written quickly and read easily:

1. Con-

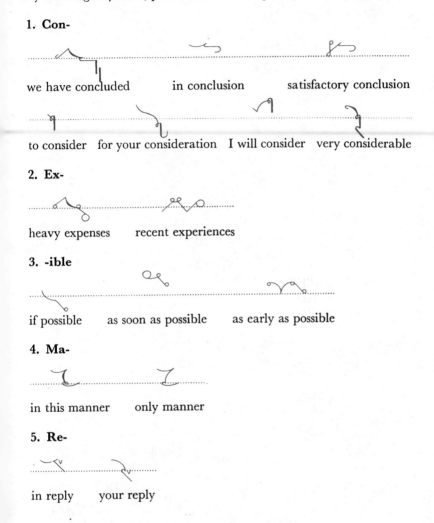

we have concluded   in conclusion   satisfactory conclusion

to consider   for your consideration   I will consider   very considerable

2. Ex-

heavy expenses   recent experiences

3. -ible

if possible   as soon as possible   as early as possible

4. Ma-

in this manner   only manner

5. Re-

in reply   your reply

PHRASING DRILL

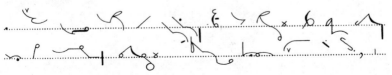

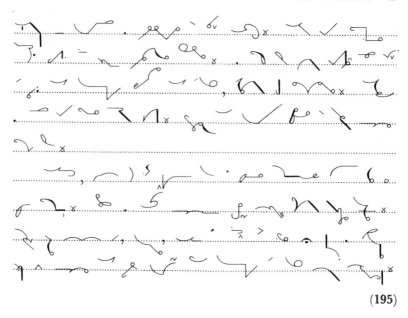

(195)

CORRESPONDENCE

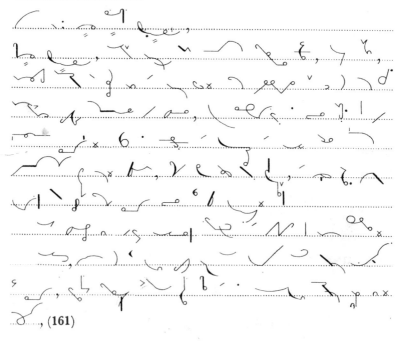

, (161)

FAR EAST HIGHLIGHTS

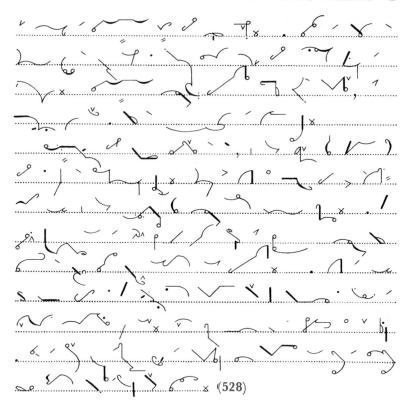

(528)

CHAPTER 6
Half-length strokes

The halving principle is used extensively in phrasing as follows:

1. It

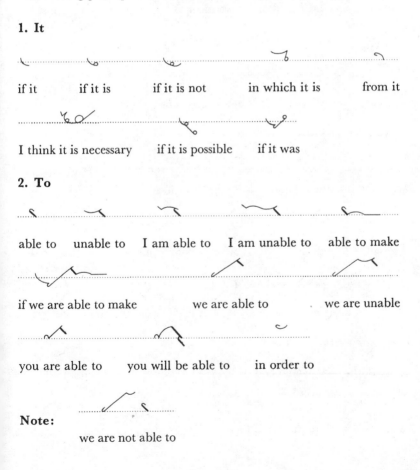

if it   if it is   if it is not   in which it is   from it

I think it is necessary   if it is possible   if it was

2. To

able to   unable to   I am able to   I am unable to   able to make

if we are able to make   we are able to   we are unable

you are able to   you will be able to   in order to

Note:

we are not able to

3. Not

(**a**) A stroke may be halved and hooked for **N** to add the word *not*:

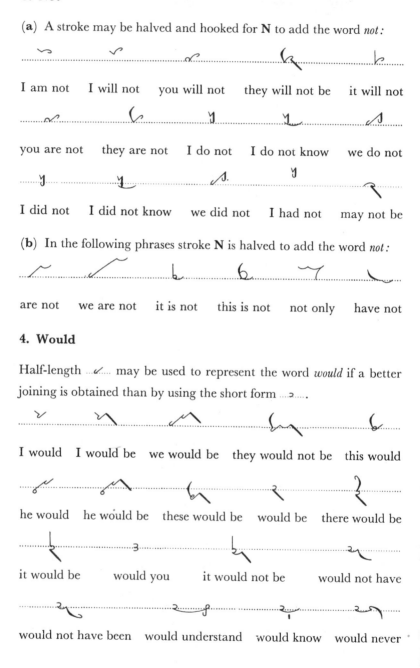

I am not   I will not   you will not   they will not be   it will not

you are not   they are not   I do not   I do not know   we do not

I did not   I did not know   we did not   I had not   may not be

(**b**) In the following phrases stroke **N** is halved to add the word *not*:

are not   we are not   it is not   this is not   not only   have not

4. Would

Half-length may be used to represent the word *would* if a better joining is obtained than by using the short form.

I would   I would be   we would be   they would not be   this would

he would   he would be   these would be   would be   there would be

it would be   would you   it would not be   would not have

would not have been   would understand   would know   would never

5. Time

In phrases the word **time** may be represented by halving the stroke preceding the word *time* and adding **M**:

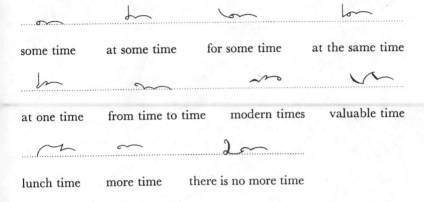

| some time | at some time | for some time | at the same time |

| at one time | from time to time | modern times | valuable time |

| lunch time | more time | there is no more time |

6. Out

The stroke preceding the word *out* is halved and the diphthong **OW** ...∧.... is added to represent the word *out*:

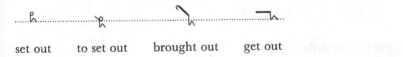

| set out | to set out | brought out | get out |

7. State/statement

Instead of writing the outline for *state* with **ST** loop, the word (or syllable) *state* may be represented by the half-length form ....ρ....:

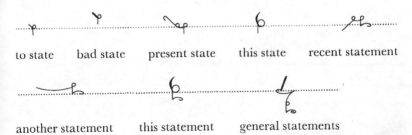

| to state | bad state | present state | this state | recent statement |

| another statement | this statement | general statements |

PHRASING DRILL

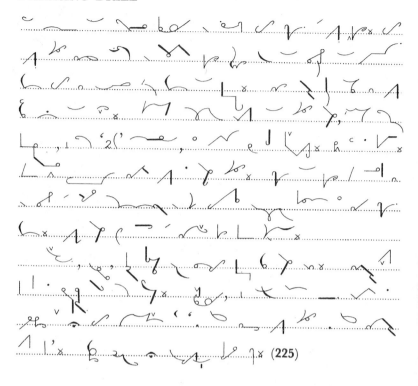

(225)

CORRESPONDENCE

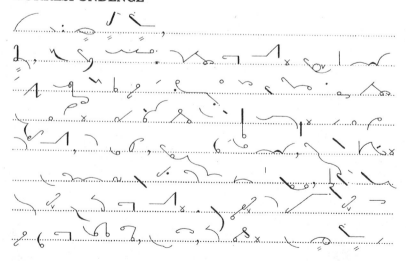

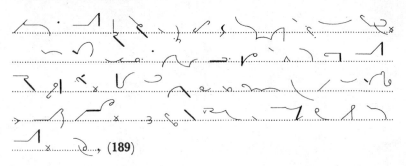

(189)

AMSTERDAM

CHAPTER 6

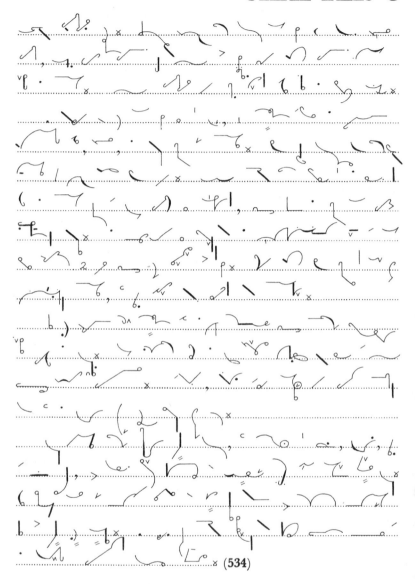

(534)

CHAPTER 7
Consonant strokes R and L

The consonant strokes upward and downward **R** are used in phrases as follows:

they are   there are   we are   you are   are you   to our   of our

if you are   these are   they were   if they were   we were

Upward L, often combined with **circle S,** is used in phrases as follows:

let us know   please let us know   let us have   please let us have

this letter   these letters   for sale   I would like   we would like

Downward L is used in phrases after **stroke N** and **stroke NG:**

any less than   no less than   something like   anything like

nothing like   any longer   no longer   anything else

PHRASING DRILL

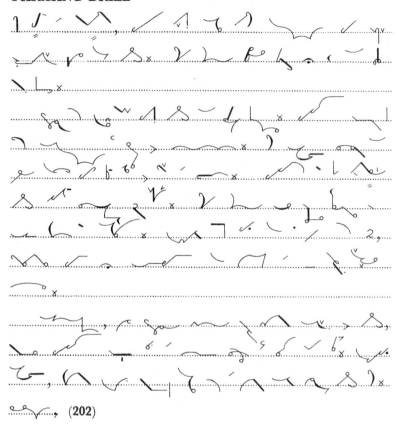

(202)

CORRESPONDENCE

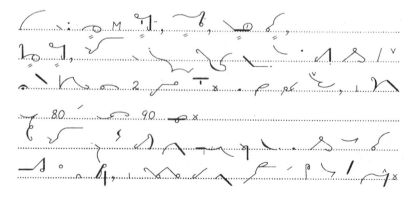

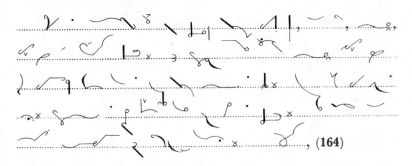

, (164)

SHORTHAND EXAMINATIONS

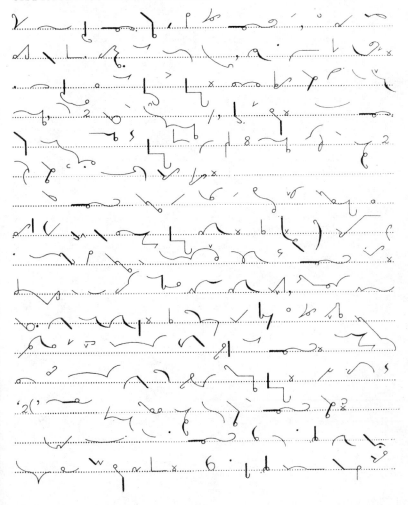

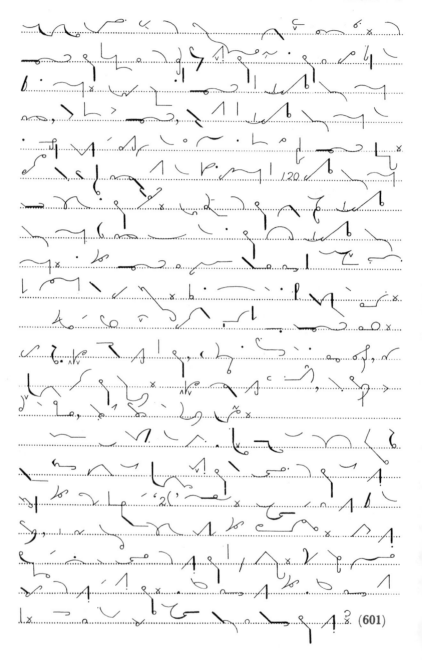

(601)

CHAPTER 8
R hook

The **R hook** to both straight and curved strokes is used in phrases to shorten many outlines. By using the **R hook** instead of an upward or downward **R,** a quicker outline is obtained:

1. Appear

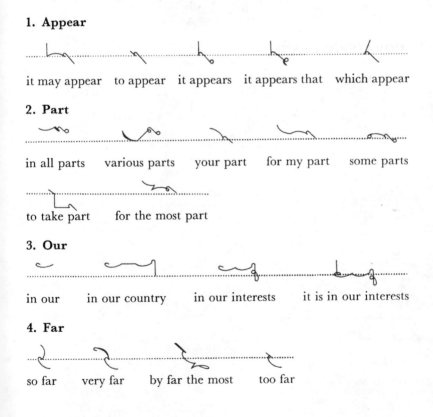

it may appear   to appear   it appears   it appears that   which appear

2. Part

in all parts   various parts   your part   for my part   some parts

to take part   for the most part

3. Our

in our   in our country   in our interests   it is in our interests

4. Far

so far   very far   by far the most   too far

PHRASING DRILL

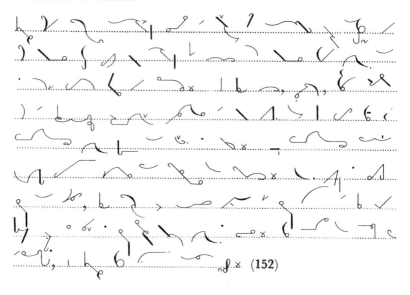

(152)

CORRESPONDENCE

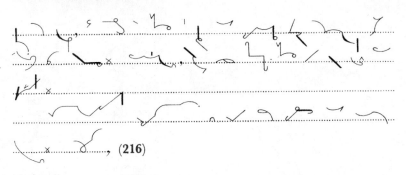

(216)

SECRETARIAL DUTIES

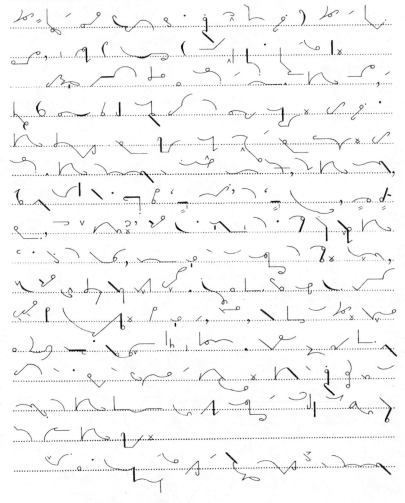

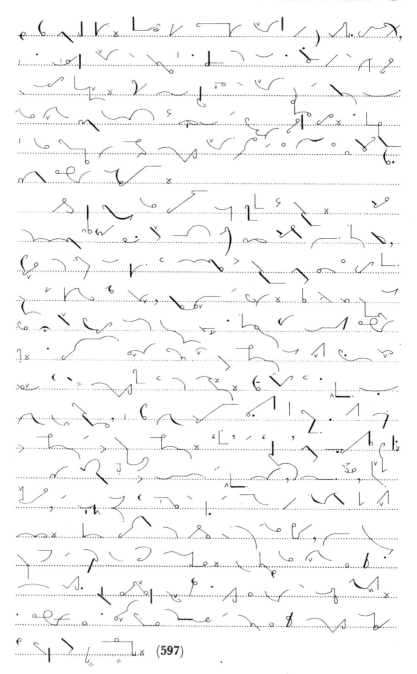

(597)

CHAPTER 9
L hook

In phrases the **L hook** is attached to strokes **T** and **B** to add the word *all*:

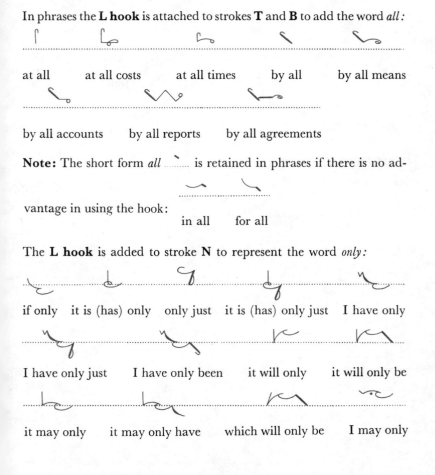

| at all | at all costs | at all times | by all | by all means |

| by all accounts | by all reports | by all agreements |

Note: The short form *all* .... is retained in phrases if there is no ad-

vantage in using the hook: in all   for all

The **L hook** is added to stroke **N** to represent the word *only*:

| if only | it is (has) only | only just | it is (has) only just | I have only |

| I have only just | I have only been | it will only | it will only be |

| it may only | it may only have | which will only be | I may only |

PHRASING DRILL

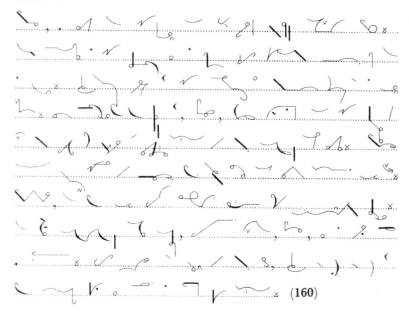

(160)

CORRESPONDENCE

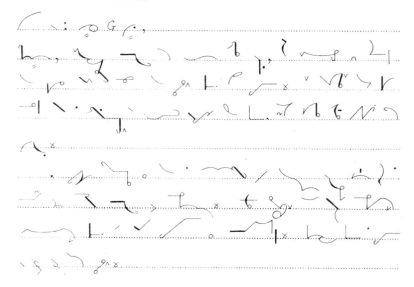

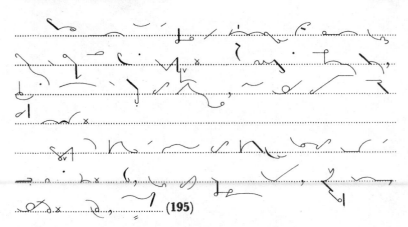

(195)

SHORTHAND SPEED DEVELOPMENT

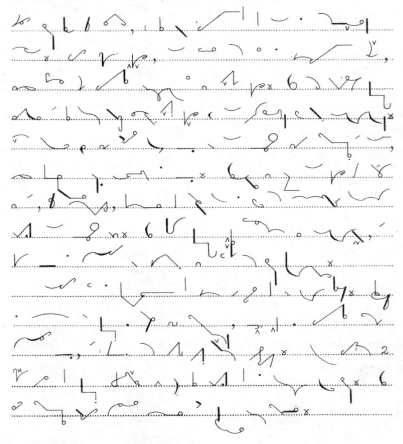

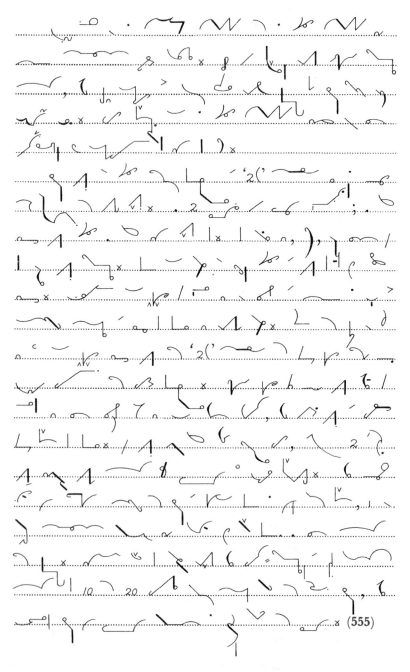

(555)

CHAPTER 10
Double-length strokes

A stroke may be doubled in phrasing for the addition of:

1. There/their

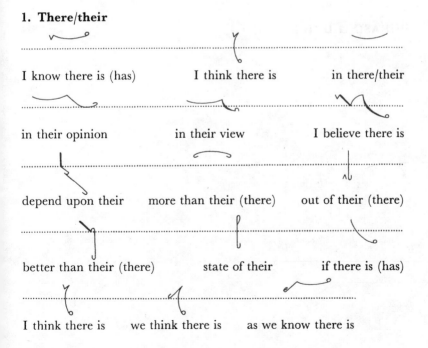

| I know there is (has) | I think there is | in there/their |

| in their opinion | in their view | I believe there is |

| depend upon their | more than their (there) | out of their (there) |

| better than their (there) | state of their | if there is (has) |

| I think there is | we think there is | as we know there is |

2. Other

some other   some other means   in some other ways   in other times

in other ways   to one another   in some other cases

3. Dear

very dear   my dear

4. Order

in order   in order that

PHRASING DRILL

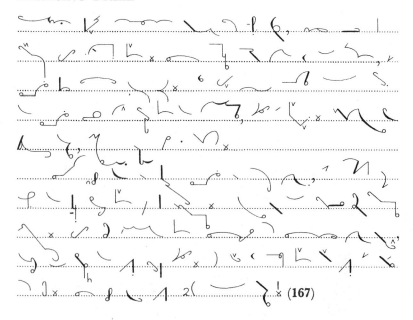

(167)

CORRESPONDENCE

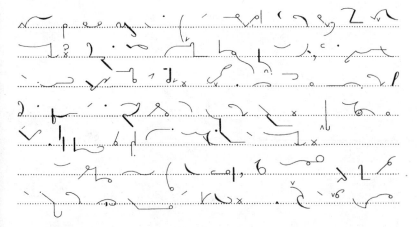

(182)

THEATRE

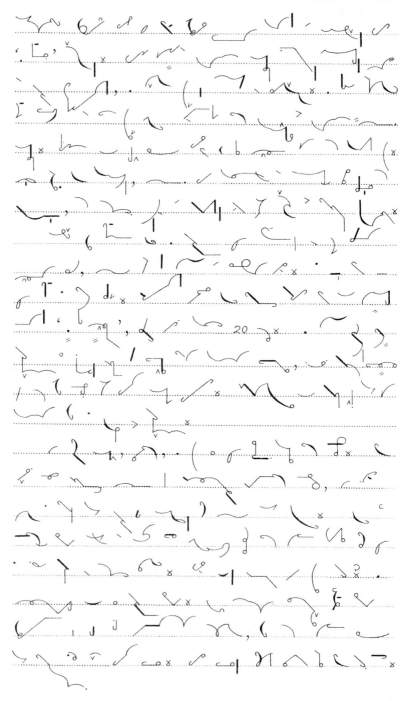

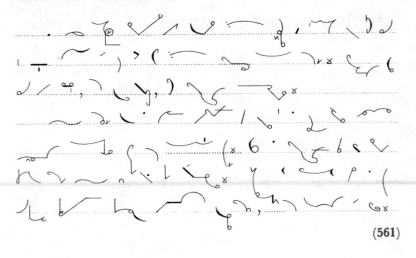

(561)

CHAPTER 11
Omission of a word

Earlier chapters have dealt with the omission of consonants, hooks and syllables. These have demonstrated that such phrases are not only very quick to write but are easy to read. A word, or a word plus a syllable, or words can be omitted from a number of phrases and yet the resulting outlines, once learned, are rapid to write and always capable of being accurately transcribed:

1. A

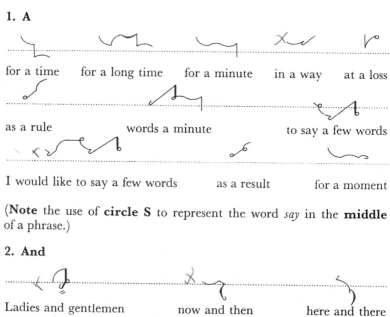

for a time	for a long time	for a minute	in a way	at a loss

as a rule	words a minute	to say a few words

I would like to say a few words	as a result	for a moment

(**Note** the use of **circle S** to represent the word *say* in the **middle** of a phrase.)

2. And

Ladies and gentlemen	now and then	here and there

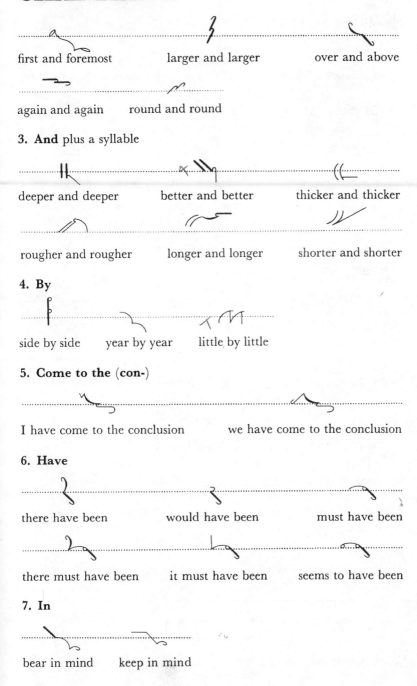

first and foremost   larger and larger   over and above

again and again   round and round

3. And plus a syllable

deeper and deeper   better and better   thicker and thicker

rougher and rougher   longer and longer   shorter and shorter

4. By

side by side   year by year   little by little

5. Come to the (con-)

I have come to the conclusion   we have come to the conclusion

6. Have

there have been   would have been   must have been

there must have been   it must have been   seems to have been

7. In

bear in mind   keep in mind

8. Of

point of view   loss of life   loss of time   as a matter of fact   first of all

9. Of the

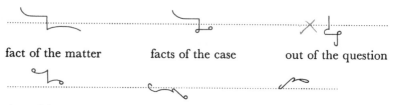

fact of the matter   facts of the case   out of the question

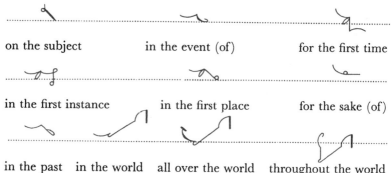

sign of the times   freedom of the press   one of the most

10. The

on the subject   in the event (of)   for the first time

in the first instance   in the first place   for the sake (of)

in the past   in the world   all over the world   throughout the world

various parts of the world   in all parts of the world

in all parts of the country   what is the matter

I am sorry to say   that is to say   in addition to   in addition to the

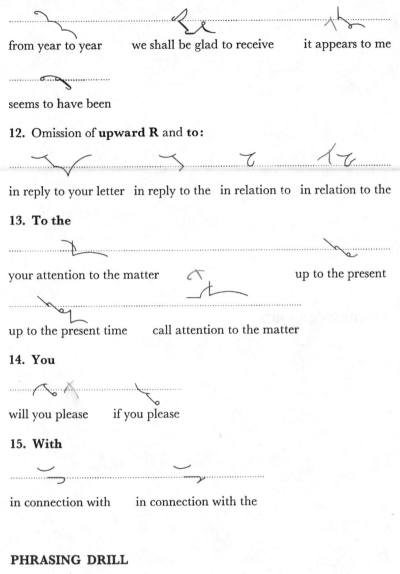

from year to year   we shall be glad to receive   it appears to me

seems to have been

12. Omission of upward R and to:

in reply to your letter   in reply to the   in relation to   in relation to the

13. To the

your attention to the matter   up to the present

up to the present time   call attention to the matter

14. You

will you please   if you please

15. With

in connection with   in connection with the

PHRASING DRILL

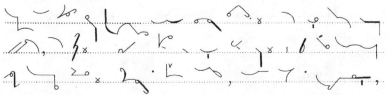

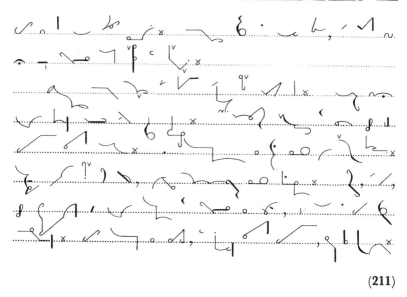

(211)

CORRESPONDENCE

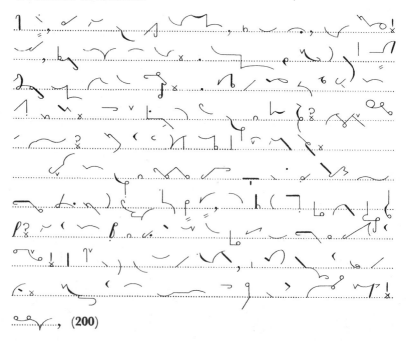

(200)

TRANSCRIPTION

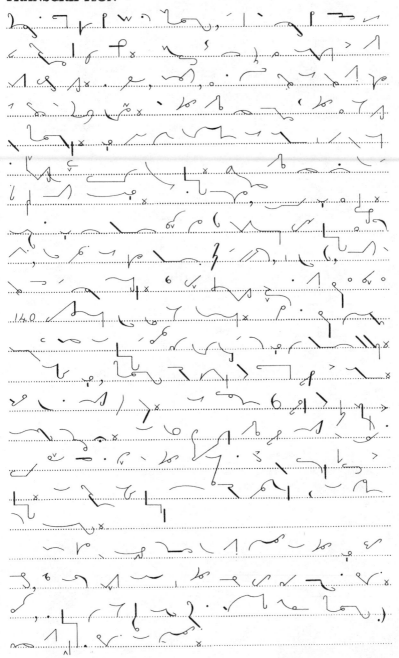

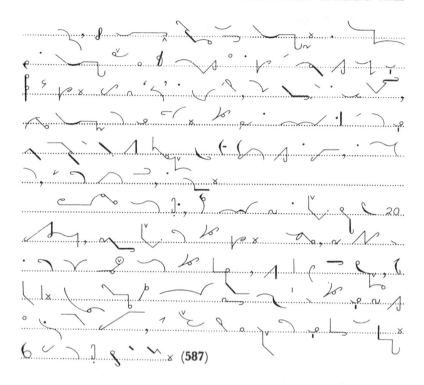

(587)

CHAPTER 12
N hook

The **N hook** may be used to represent the words *been, than, own,* in phrasing as follows:

1. Been

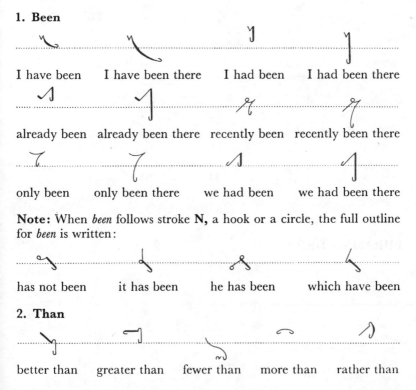

I have been   I have been there   I had been   I had been there

already been   already been there   recently been   recently been there

only been   only been there   we had been   we had been there

Note: When *been* follows stroke **N,** a hook or a circle, the full outline for *been* is written:

has not been   it has been   he has been   which have been

2. Than

better than   greater than   fewer than   more than   rather than

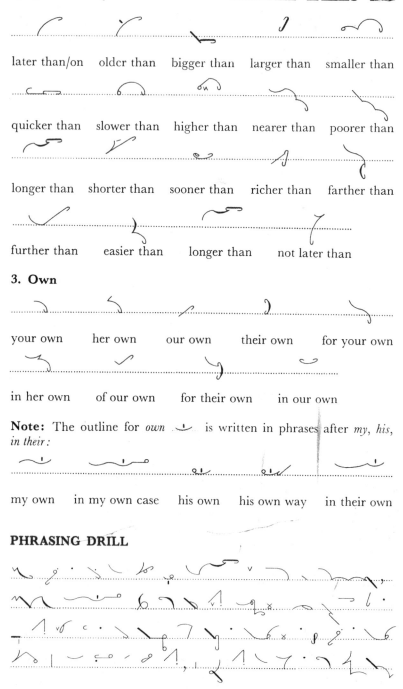

later than/on   older than   bigger than   larger than   smaller than

quicker than   slower than   higher than   nearer than   poorer than

longer than   shorter than   sooner than   richer than   farther than

further than   easier than   longer than   not later than

3. Own

your own   her own   our own   their own   for your own

in her own   of our own   for their own   in our own

Note: The outline for *own* is written in phrases after *my, his, in their:*

my own   in my own case   his own   his own way   in their own

PHRASING DRILL

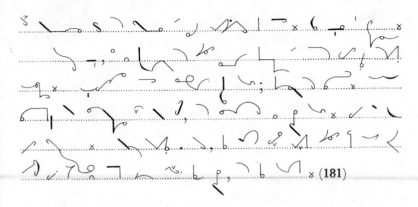

(181)

CORRESPONDENCE

(179)

WORKING ABROAD

(547)

CHAPTER 13
F and V hook

The **F/V hook** may represent the words *have, of* and *off*. It also takes the place of the stroke **V** in phrases containing the word *event:*

1. Have

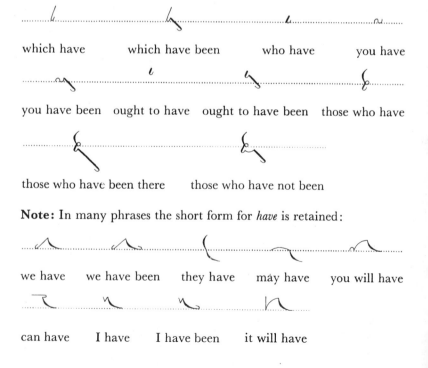

which have   which have been   who have   you have

you have been   ought to have   ought to have been   those who have

those who have been there   those who have not been

Note: In many phrases the short form for *have* is retained:

we have   we have been   they have   may have   you will have

can have   I have   I have been   it will have

2. Of

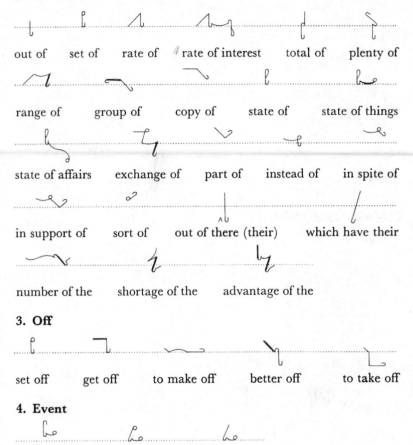

out of   set of   rate of   rate of interest   total of   plenty of

range of   group of   copy of   state of   state of things

state of affairs   exchange of   part of   instead of   in spite of

in support of   sort of   out of there (their)   which have their

number of the   shortage of the   advantage of the

3. Off

set off   get off   to make off   better off   to take off

4. Event

at all events   such events   which events

PHRASING DRILL

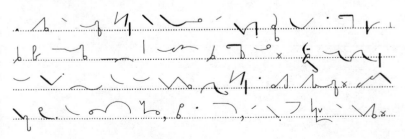

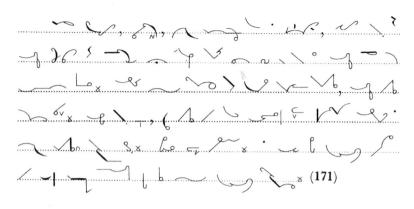

(171)

CORRESPONDENCE

W.C.2.B. 5.P.B.,

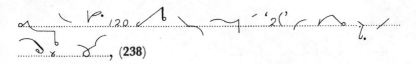

(238)

GARDENING

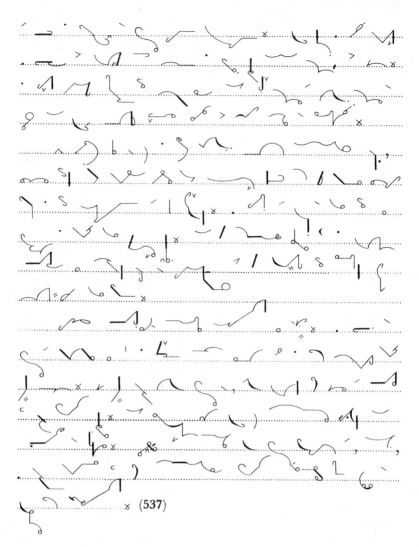

(537)

CHAPTER 14
Shun hook
Vocalization in phrases
Disjoining in phrases

SHUN HOOK

The **Shun** hook is used to represent the word *ocean* in some phrases:

Atlantic Ocean   Pacific Ocean   Arctic Ocean

The combination **circle S-shun** is used to represent the word *association* in phrases:

Medical Association   Football Association   Automobile Association

your association   Trade Association

VOCALIZATION IN PHRASES

Certain phrases are identical in outline and therefore it is necessary to vocalize *one* of them:

at least   at last   by any means   by no means   you will say

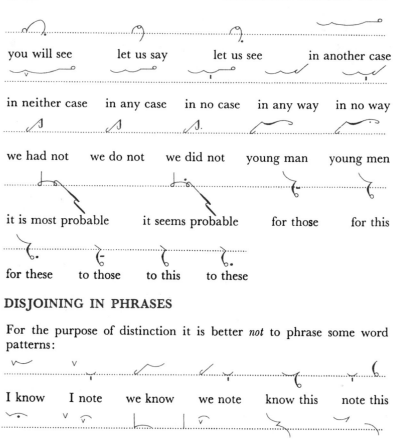

you will see   let us say   let us see   in another case

in neither case   in any case   in no case   in any way   in no way

we had not   we do not   we did not   young man   young men

it is most probable   it seems probable   for those   for this

for these   to those   to this   to these

DISJOINING IN PHRASES

For the purpose of distinction it is better *not* to phrase some word patterns:

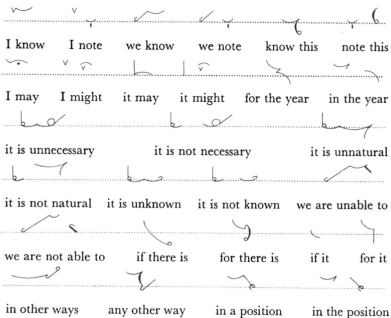

I know   I note   we know   we note   know this   note this

I may   I might   it may   it might   for the year   in the year

it is unnecessary   it is not necessary   it is unnatural

it is not natural   it is unknown   it is not known   we are unable to

we are not able to   if there is   for there is   if it   for it

in other ways   any other way   in a position   in the position

PHRASING DRILL

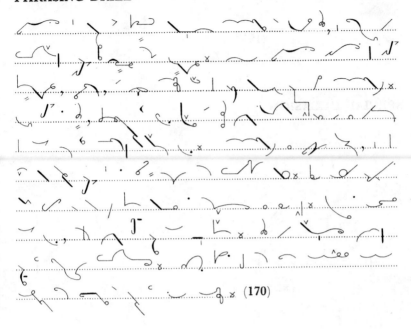

(170)

CORRESPONDENCE

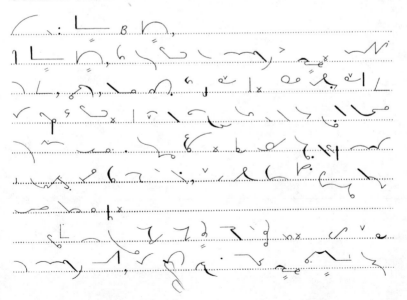

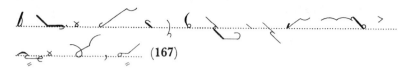

(167)

SPECIAL OCCASION

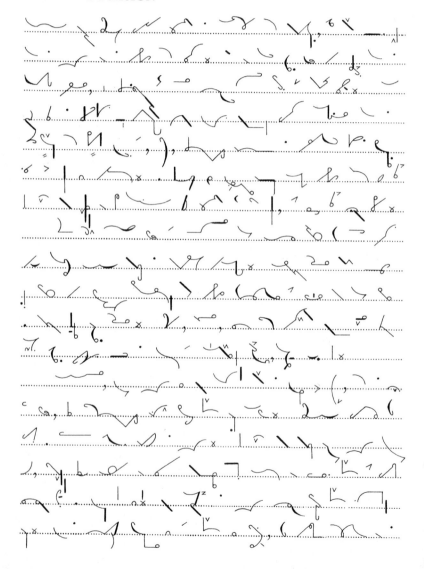

(569)

CHAPTER 15
Disjoining for CON, COM

The sounds **CON** and **COM** are indicated in phrases by omitting the **CON/COM** dot and writing the stroke following these sounds close to the preceding outline:

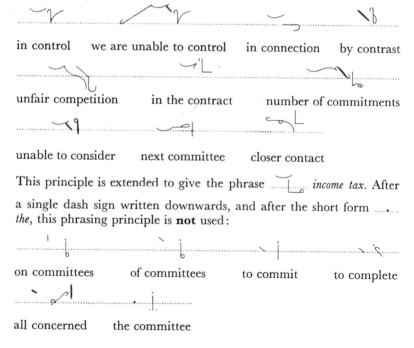

in control   we are unable to control   in connection   by contrast

unfair competition   in the contract   number of commitments

unable to consider   next committee   closer contact

This principle is extended to give the phrase .... *income tax*. After a single dash sign written downwards, and after the short form ....•.... *the*, this phrasing principle is **not** used:

on committees   of committees   to commit   to complete

all concerned   the committee

PHRASING DRILL

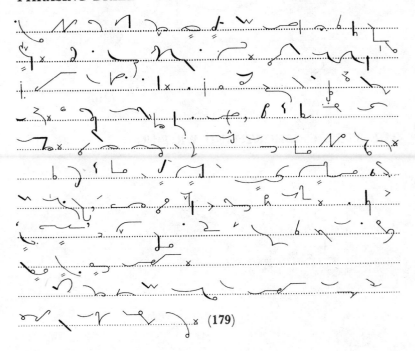

(179)

CORRESPONDENCE

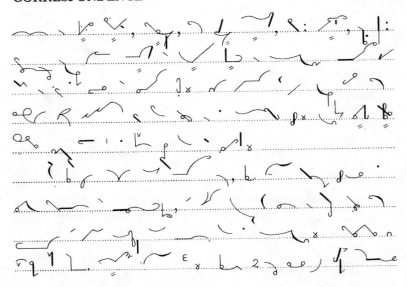

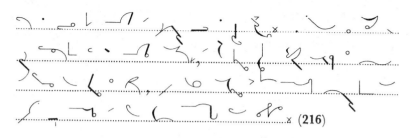

(216)

THE SKILL OF SHORTHAND WRITING

(548)

CHAPTER 1
Tick The
Diphthongs I and U

Phrasing Drill

Thank you for the way in which you attended to / the order I left with you yesterday. This is the / best service I have had and you are to be / congratulated.

In the course of my telephone conversation with your / secretary she informed me that you will be going to / the conference next week. If you meet the company president / would you please give him my good wishes. The week / you are going to be at the conference happens to / be the end of the financial year for me and / I shall not be able to spare the time. Would / you let me have the results of the voting when / you return to the office. I will be very interested / to have your views on the decisions taken.

If you / can spare the time perhaps I can have lunch with / you next month? Would you let me know and I / will make a reservation. If you like I will be / able to collect you by car and I suggest we / lunch out of town. (**174**)

Correspondence

Dear Sir, Thank you for your enquiry about the new / 'Villa in the Sun' project which the company is about / to launch. The company has just been formed to meet / the tremendous demand for this form of investment. The directors / of the company all have the necessary professional expertise to / deal with the many complexities of investing abroad and, as / you will see from the enclosed brochure, each one of / them holds a prominent position in public office. It is / very difficult to convey to clients the outstanding qualities of / these properties by the means of a brochure.

If you / are seriously considering purchasing one of the villas, it is / the policy of the company to make the suggestion that / you take advantage of the special offer inspection flight before / the agreement is signed. In this way you will be / able to see the property and not simply have to / rely on the word of the seller. You can make / the final decision on your own judgement which is the / very best way to do something as important as this. / Yours faithfully, (**182**)

Qualifications

When you are taking training in the secretarial skills it / is the usual thing to enter for some examinations at / the end of the course. Such examinations should be considered / in the correct light and you should have the right / attitude towards them. They are a measurement of what has / been achieved, and of what progress has been made, at / the conclusion of the training programme. Contrary to the opinion / of the candidates they are not special means of torture / dreamed up by the teaching staff! If you can stand / back a little and look at the course you are / attending in an objective way, I think you will agree / that some form of measuring your success is very useful. /

Just as important, of course, is the necessity to prove / to your would-be employer that you are the right / person for the job, and during the course of an / interview this can be easily done by producing to the / interviewer your certificates. Your potential as an employee will be / assessed from the results of any examinations you have taken, / and also a note may be made of examinations you / have sat but for which the results are not yet / known.

In the course of changing jobs these qualifications from / school or college are still very useful, and even more / impressive are the additional certificates you have obtained as the / result of attending evening or day-release classes. It is / a good point to keep in mind that studying does / not necessarily stop when you leave school or college. Many / secretarial students add to their speed in both shorthand and / typewriting by attending evening classes and it is particularly useful / to do this immediately you commence work. Set your sights / on certain speeds and make the decision to achieve these / aims within a given time.

Many secretaries return to the / classroom after several years of work experience to study for / examinations leading to a teaching qualification and this can be / done on a full-time or part-time basis. These / exponents of the secretarial skills make excellent teachers of shorthand, / typewriting and office practice, because they are able to bring / their invaluable experience into the teaching situation.

When preparing for / examinations you will receive guidance from the teacher about the / level of examination you should be taking. Just because you / were once writing at 120 words a / minute when drilling a sentence or phrase, does not mean / you are ready to take a test lasting several minutes / at the same speed. If you can write for a / sustained period of time at 120 words / a minute, and if you also have a reserve speed / to write for at least a minute well above that / speed, then you will be able to enter for the / 120 examination with confidence.

Try comparing yourself / with a car. A car has a cruising speed at / which it can be driven for long periods of time / with total comfort for the passengers and little strain on / the engine. When necessary the speed can be increased up / to the maximum of which the car is capable, but / only for short periods of time. You should be entering / an examination at your cruising speed, which will leave you / with your 'reserve tank' to call upon if needed during / the examination. (562)

CHAPTER 2

He
Hope
Tick H

Phrasing Drill

Mr. Henry Hill has been with this firm for five / years, and he is regarded by everyone for whom he / works as highly competent. Before joining us in research he / was employed for a long period of time by a / large manufacturing firm.

He knows how to handle every aspect / of this work and if he is faced with a / problem he will always suggest some excellent ways of overcoming / it. His colleagues know he can be called upon for / assistance at any time. We hope he will stay with / us for many years, but we do know that he / is applying for a post with your company as he / is anxious to move to your area of the country. / He will be nearer to his wife's family and it / will be easier for her to look after her elderly / parents.

If he is successful in his application we hope / he will be happy in his new situation, and we / hope that you will understand when we say to him / that he will always have a job waiting for him / should he decide to return here. (**186**)

Correspondence

Memo to all staff, from the Branch Manager, subject: FLEXIBLE WORKING HOURS, today's date:

The Managing Director has asked me to ascertain how many / of the staff would be interested in a work programme / of flexible hours. He said he is prepared to introduce / such a scheme in the immediate

81

future if he can / be sure that the staff are keen to support it. / What he is anxious to avoid is imposing such a / radical change on an unwilling staff. I will ask him / if he will let you have full details of his / plans and I hope you will give this matter your / serious consideration during the course of the next few days. / The Managing Director has said that he will be pleased / to answer any questions about these proposals at a meeting / that he will be arranging to take place next week. / After hearing your questions and general views on this subject / he will make the final decision.

I hope you will / be able to reach agreement among yourselves on this issue / before the meeting takes place. (**165**)

On Being Employed

Let us consider the situation of being employed for the / first time, and for the purpose of this article let / us refer to the employer as 'he' and the employee / as 'she' although we all appreciate that there are female / employers and male employees.

First of all, how high will / the standards be that the employer can expect or demand / of his new secretarial worker? He will certainly expect a / standard high enough to cope with the routine work of / any office, and more if the applicant at the interview / claims to have very high speeds in shorthand and typing. / If he is paying extra money for particular qualifications an / employer will rightly expect that member of staff to have / such qualifications and be able to use them effectively in / the work situation. For example, if he knows that he / is a rapid dictator he will want a secretary with / an above-average shorthand speed, or if a foreign language / is involved he will want a bilingual secretary.

Even without / any special qualifications being called for, an employer will always / be looking for a precise and accurate worker. There is / nothing more annoying for him than having to check through / the work of a shorthand-typist or secretary word by / word knowing that there is every chance of finding numerous / errors. I hope you will be shocked to think that / such a step is necessary. The fact is that many / new employees are so anxious to impress their boss, as / well as everyone around them, that they rush through the / work, do not check errors, and the result is that / far too many mistakes are made and, even worse, are / not detected and corrected. What an employer expects to do / is to glance over a finished piece of work and / sign it with confidence, knowing that his member of staff / is an accurate and careful worker. So, take extra care / with all the work you will do for him on / first being employed. He will be much more impressed with / your efforts if you do not have to repeat jobs / because of careless mistakes, even though you may take a / little longer than might be expected in the early days / of employment.

Good timekeeping is another thing which your employer / will expect. It may be that you will be the / first person to arrive each day at the office—in / fact, you might have to 'open-up' and put the / whole place into operation. It is important that he can / absolutely rely on you to do this. He will then / be able to concentrate on the other aspects of his / work in the knowledge that his staff will be looking / after the just as important routine matters.

The word 'routine' / is very common in the business world and you will / find that you have to settle into a very definite / pattern or routine of work. At first you may feel / that the jobs you will be given to do are / not very interesting or important. Your future within the organisation / will largely be determined on how well you perform those / early tasks. Anything which has to be done should be / done to the very best of your ability. No-one / can defend a poor and inadequate piece of work by / saying, 'I did not think it was important'.

I hope / you will be able to accept this advice and put / it to good use. As an employee you will be / paid to carry out these office duties and I / hope your employer will always consider that he is getting good / value. (**601**)

CHAPTER 3
Circle S
Omission of a consonant

Phrasing Drill (a) ,

It is necessary for you to take steps to practise / all new phrases very thoroughly. You should write a new / phrase slowly once only, and that is the first time. / After that it is really important for you to write / as fast as you can. It seems necessary for me / to say a few words about drilling because it is / well known that better results can be obtained, and satisfactory / records of progress have been reported after students have listened / to me. Each phrase must be drilled very well, that / is written many times as a single phrase, or within / a group of phrases, until it is totally under your / control otherwise you will have poor results. In fact, I / trust that each phrase will be drilled so well that / it becomes a part of you. Please do not take / exception to my suggestion that the last time you practised / the phrase you did not concentrate enough on what you / were doing. (**162**)

Phrasing Drill (b)

Past experience shows that the best time to practise shorthand / is when there is peace and quiet and there is / nothing to distract you from the work you have to / do. Satisfactory results will follow a carefully planned routine. With / phrasing you may not see any speed development at once / because it is a gradual thing. It is important to / remember that the phrasing principles are of the greatest importance / and these should be kept in mind as you drill / the individual phrases.

Please accept my best wishes for your / success. My own teacher has said over the past few / years that in his opinion students always achieve some measure / of success. Depend upon us for the best advice and / please make a point of drilling every day. However, we / realize that some phrases are used less frequently than others. / We do not write 'Prime Minister' or 'past year' as / often as we use a phrase like 'in your last / letter'. (**161**)

Correspondence

Letter to: Mr James Handley, Manager, Natural Cosmetics Limited,

Dear Sir, For several years now, in fact since we / left school, my friend and I have been considering careers / in cosmetics. At the time we left school there were / no opportunities to enter this kind of work. As we / went straight from school to an insurance office, where we / have been employed as clerks for the past three years, / our ambitions have unfortunately not yet been realized. We are / still very keen to train and specialize in the cosmetics / field, and we trust that you can advise us.

We / understand that there is a training school run by your / company in the West End of London. As we are / keen to come into the cosmetics industry, we wish to / know the best time to apply for a place as / we cannot leave our present jobs at a minute's notice. / We also wish to know what the career prospects are / with your company for successful trainees.

I do not think / it is necessary at this stage to give you any / personal details other than to state that we are both / 19 years of age and have five O-Levels each. / Any advice you will be able to give us would / be very much appreciated. Yours faithfully, (**206**)

Flying Today

Few airlines have had satisfactory results in the past few / years; in fact many are running at a loss. People / only fly when it is necessary because it is no / longer regarded as exciting. For several years, there has been / fierce competition between airlines and as far as customers are / concerned it has been beneficial with price reductions and improved / service. Trans-Atlantic flights must be some of the most / popular and a look at a typical crossing will inform / us about general conditions.

Most of the airlines take steps / to help us pass the time as enjoyably as we / can. During the long flight, drinks, snacks and full meals, / hot and cold, are provided. The very large jumbo jets / are divided into sections so that you are really unaware / of the enormous size of the craft, and huge sums / of money are spent on interior decoration and in providing / comfortable and usually adjustable seats.

First-class passengers, usually few / in number, as we know pay considerably more for the / flight in return for which they receive extra space, a / wider choice of food, free drinks and sometimes even a / separate lounge area in which they can sit or walk / around.

For several years airlines have been offering a choice / of smoking and non-smoking areas as well as a / choice of films. Whilst cruising leisurely you have an opportunity / to view a recent release or sometimes even a pre-release / film. When there is a choice it is usually between / family life or animal life films, and one suitable for / adults only. On some flights the showing of the films / is staggered and you can, as a result, see both / features.

After take-off the cabin crew at once demonstrate / life-saving equipment and emergency procedures. Drinks are available and / a menu is distributed in advance of the main meal / being served, resulting in a hectic time for the stewards / and stewardesses when everyone seems to be requiring their services / at once. In fact during this particular flight the cabin / staff seem to be fully occupied tending to the needs / of their passengers just as fast as they can.

After / the main meal is over and the trays have been / cleared away the film is shown. Throughout this time there / have been communications from the flight-deck, usually from the / captain himself, to inform us about the speed and height / of the aircraft, scheduled time of arrival and weather conditions / at the destination airport. For those not wanting to view / the film there is a wide choice of stereo music / which can be heard through the headsets which are distributed / and which plug into a socket in the side of / the seat. Newspapers, magazines and often notepaper and post cards / are available as additional 'time killers'.

By this stage the / journey is more than half over. Once again drinks are / served and a light meal in the form of afternoon / tea during day flights and breakfast during over-night flights. / Then there is just sufficient time to complete the forms / required by the customs and immigration officials before we are / asked to fasten our seat belts and the jet begins / its descent to an international airport on the other side / of the ocean. (**543**)

CHAPTER 4
Ses circle
Omission of a hook

Phrasing Drill

It is said that correcting typewritten errors presents problems to /
some students, yet with so many aids available and so / much having
been said on this subject there should not / be any difficulty. It is
certain that a good clean / correction is as easy or as difficult as you
wish / to make it. There is only one way to get / a good correction and
that is done with a clean / eraser. It is suggested that a soft eraser
should be / used first to remove the top layer of ink if / a new typing
ribbon is in the machine, and then / a firm eraser should be applied
with just as much / pressure as is necessary to clear the remainder of
the / ink impression.

As we know there are many other correction / aids. As well as
specially coated papers which blank out / the error when inserted
between the ribbon and paper, there / are liquids to paint out errors.
As we feel there / is little difference between them, it is a matter
of / personal choice and a satisfactory result still depends on how / it is
done. Remember, however, that a clean correction on / the carbon
copy is equally important. I trust that these / points will be of some
help to you and that / as soon as we can we shall be able to / watch you
put this advice into practice. (**227**)

Correspondence

Letter to: Miss Susan Johnson,

Dear Susan, Thank you so much for all the work / you and your friends
did on Saturday on behalf of / the Society. I am delighted to tell you

that the / amount collected is a record for this city. No other / town or city has had a collection as satisfactory as / this, and it simply must be that you and your / team worked extremely hard. In second place this year has / been the collection made in Georgetown. As usual on our / collecting days, it rained, and I was most impressed by / the enthusiasm and dedication of everyone who turned out to / help.

It is now certain that the plans proposed for / the Society within the next year can be carried out / subject to funds being available. It is satisfactory to begin / a new year knowing that all obligations can be met. / This has been made possible by the efforts of you / and your team and similar helpers throughout the country. The / Society is greatly indebted to you. Yours sincerely, (**168**)

Antiques

There seems to be an increasing number of antique shops / opening, and suddenly people have become very conscious about objects / from the past. Informative articles appear regularly in newspapers and / magazines, books on this subject seem to be published each / month, and the public is being well educated about antiques / through the media of television and radio. Why is it / then that everyone has suddenly 'discovered' antiques?

First of all, / let us consider the definition of an antique. The connoisseur / would insist that to be classified as an antique an / article must be at least 100 years old. On / the other hand, people do collect things not nearly as / old as that simply because they find them attractive. The / market value of an item is greatly influenced by the / law of supply and demand. When only a comparatively few / items were manufactured or hand-made, and a great many / people on the other side of the world may now / want to own one of them, the scarcity rating will / raise the price and there could be many overseas buyers. /

For some collectors, whether they are interested in paintings, silver / or porcelain, it is a way of saving for their / old age or one way of combating inflation. It is / suggested that rare objects steadily increase in value, but there / are some problems in collecting. Fashions come and go in / this field just as much as in others. The works / of a particular painter long-since dead will suddenly be / in demand and pictures painted by him, and preferably signed / and dated, will soar in price. Beautiful pieces of Georgian / silverware, in spite of their age and rarity, also vary / in value according to the world price of silver on / the metal markets. Today it is very fashionable to collect / anything Victorian; tomorrow such items might be in second place / if a new fashion appears.

88

Other people start collecting because / they buy one particular item and like it so much / that they collect others similar to it whenever they have / the opportunity and can afford to purchase. A genuine antique / is not necessarily expensive. Indeed a large number of articles / may be in circulation and this is the reason the / price is as low as it is.

There is something / fascinating about a shop which only sells things from bygone / days. Looking round one of these establishments anyone with a / lively imagination can be very easily transported back in time. / What impresses most people is the magnificent workmanship of articles / which were made before mass-production was known. Furniture which / has been hand-carved has a very special quality and / beauty about it, and there is an extra depth to / the shine of old oak and mahogany. So interested in / the goods are many of the potential customers that they / never reach the point of making a purchase, but antique / dealers seem to possess an abundance of patience and this / is necessary if they are to be successful in business. /

Every Saturday in London an extraordinary market presents an incredible / display of antiques. Shoppers from home and abroad may be / seen converging on Portobello Road. Amateurs and professionals enjoy the / hustle and bustle of this highly specialized market and collectors / from this side of the world meet up with enthusiasts / from abroad. As has been stated, collecting antiques is growing / in popularity.

(562)

CHAPTER 5
St loop
Omission of a syllable

Phrasing Drill

The final figures for last year are poor compared with / those for the last few years. This is the first / time we have had to meet such unexpected heavy expenses. / At first appearance it may seem like bad planning, but / nobody could forecast the recent experience of high inflation. In / reply to our critics I can say we did act / to protect ourselves as soon as possible. The very first / step will be to reduce the costs of lighting and / heating in the factory as well as in the offices, / and this will be done as early as possible. In / this manner the cost of our products can be held. / Please let us have any further suggestions of possible economies / from the staff.

In conclusion, let me say that the / outlook for a first-class organization like this is still / very good. As fast as the national economic situation improves / there will be better results for this company. Your reply / to this memo should, if possible, include an account of / the efforts made during the last few days to consider / how economies in the use of fuel in our factory / and offices may be implemented. **(195)**

Correspondence

Letter to: Miss Sandra Stephenson,

Dear Miss Stephenson, In reply to your enquiry about career / prospects with this company, for which I thank you, I / am certain I can be of assistance to you and / to your friend. From recent experience I would say your / chances of employment within the organization are first-class, after / successfully completing a course of training at our cosmetic school. / This is an expanding company and vacancies and new appointments / occur regularly throughout the year. Just now, there are several / posts being advertised, and most of these will be filled / by students from the school course that is just finishing. /

In the first instance you should complete the enclosed application / form and return it to me as soon as possible. /

In conclusion, let me say that if you wish to / have any further information before enrolling with the school, please / contact the personnel department of the company at this address / and an interview can be arranged to suit you. Yours / sincerely, (**161**)

Far East Highlights

My itinerary was to be five days in Bangkok, five / days in Hong Kong and four days in Singapore, and / I was very excited at the prospect of seeing three / different countries on my first visit to the Far East. / The flight from London to Bangkok, including a refuelling stop / in the Persian Gulf, took some seventeen hours.

No place / in the world can look very attractive at / 0700 hours after such a long journey and Bangkok was / no exception. In fact at first appearance it looked more / than a little dusty and dirty and even at that / early hour the traffic seemed to be ridiculously heavy and / congested. I learned later that this city has one of / the worst traffic problems in the world.

After a quick / sleep I was ready to start exploring. My first impressions / were not quickly dispelled and it was not until later / the following day that the real magic and beauty of / this fascinating place began to affect me. The magnificent temples / have to be seen to be believed and even those / which have fallen into disrepair are very beautiful. First thing / on my last morning I visited the floating market where / the sellers offered every kind of commodity from their boats. / There were many lovely sights to see in the city / and throughout Thailand, but before long I realised that what / is so special about this country is the people. I / think they are the most beautiful in the world.

The / flight to Hong Kong by Thai International Airways was first- / class with the best cabin service I have had on / any journey. How different Hong Kong was, but how immediate / was my response to this incredible place. The first thing / to impress me, and I cannot explain my surprise about / this, was the majesty of the whole area. The greenery / of the hills all around was quite unexpected but the / magnificence of the great harbour lived up to all expectations. / That first ride on the Star Ferry between Kowloon on / the mainland and

Hong Kong Island was most exciting. The / hustle and bustle of so many thousands of people in / such a comparatively small area was amazingly gentle and orderly. / Hong Kong must be the world's greatest shopping paradise, and / the gourmet will find the best of international and local / dishes.

Singapore was the biggest surprise of all, but for / the first time on this journey there was a touch / of sentimental disappointment. So much of the old has given / way to the ultra-modern new but for the inhabitants / this must be the answer to many dreams. The large / housing developments in and around the city are really splendid / and the city centre must have the best selection of / beautiful hotels to be found anywhere in the world. The / old and new blend together when a large open-air / car park by day becomes a fascinating and lively market- / place each night. My trip came to a satisfactory conclusion / as I tasted the hot and spicy foods and tropical / fruits and purchased some bargains in precious and semi-precious / stones that were being offered by the salesmen. (**528**)

CHAPTER 6
Half-length strokes

Phrasing Drill

In order to make any progress it is necessary to / concentrate when drilling and reading outlines. When reading shorthand you / must endeavour to absorb outlines so that you will not / have any hesitancy in recalling them when you next hear / them in dictation. You will not be able to do / so unless you read with this aim in mind. Challenge / yourself to read any shorthand passage, not only from your / textbooks, but from '2000' magazine, as rapidly as if / it had been typewritten. Set out with a target. Check / how quickly you are able to read a passage of / shorthand. Drill any outlines which caused you to hesitate and / always remember to say the words to yourself at the / same time as you are drilling them. Read the passage / through again and you will find it will not take / so long.

Finally, if it is possible, it would be / advantageous to have someone dictate this passage to you. You / should be able to write it at a speed considerably / above your average. I do not think it is necessary, / but nevertheless I am going to repeat a recent statement / I made one lunchtime that 'the faster you can read / shorthand the faster you will be able to write it'. / This statement would not have been made if we did / not know it was true. (**225**)

Correspondence

Letter to: Mr John Black,

Dear Sir, I have pleasure in enclosing your replacement credit / card. Please sign it immediately and read the instructions about / its use and safe-keeping as I am not able / to promise a second replacement if this one is lost. / You are solely responsible for all debts incurred. Should you / lose your card, or if it is stolen, please inform / this office immediately, preferably by telephone.

If from time to / time you have to be away from home on business, / it would be of benefit for your wife to have / her own credit card. The busy housewife or working wife / can use these credit facilities as much as, if not / more than, her husband. If Mrs Black should require a / card it would be possible to issue one without the / formality of completing another application form.

I am also enclosing / a leaflet giving details of how your credit card can / be used abroad. Additional information will be sent to you / from time to time if there are any alterations to / the currency regulations. Would you please be kind enough to / acknowledge the safe receipt of your card. Yours faithfully, (**189**)

Amsterdam

Amsterdam is a city of surprises and unexpected delights. What / is not surprising is that its reputation has spread throughout / the world and it has become a very cosmopolitan place. / It would be very difficult to stroll through the city / centre without meeting, or recognizing visitors from many different parts / of the world. In the height of the summer great / throngs of people arrive by jet at the international airport / every hour, and buses, trains and motor-cars converge upon / the city. The Dutch cope with this influx very well / and the Government Tourist Bureau guarantees to find accommodation for / everyone at prices to suit the individual's pocket, whether or / not advance reservations have been made.

For all English-speaking / visitors it is a tremendous comfort to find that the / English language is a compulsory subject in all schools, and / everywhere they go it is possible to find someone who / can speak in English. Everyone involved in tourism speaks this / language fluently and several others besides, and consequently there are / no language barriers in hotels, restaurants, shops or on tourist / excursions in and around the city. As a result you / will find a very large proportion of the visitors come / from the United States, Canada, Britain and the Commonwealth countries. /

A map of the city looks like a spider's web. / The centre is the old city, once walled, and the / many strands of the web are the canals and rivers / forming an incredible waterways system. It is impossible to move / very far in the city without having to cross water, / indeed when walking down many of the city streets you / are also walking along the side of a canal. Many / waterways are tree-lined and this adds a special enchantment. /

The best way to see any city is on foot, / but Amsterdam offers a unique alternative and that is, of / course, a boat trip on the canals. Several different firms / have very comfortable launches which leave almost every hour. Nothing / can be more pleasant on a sunny day than a / canal tour and if the weather is unsettled, you can / take a trip in one of the glass-domed boats. / An excellent commentary is provided by a multi-lingual guide / and in the space of one or two hours you / can see the highlights of the city. There are also / several trips at night through the illuminated canals, with cheese / and wine being served by candlelight.

It is easy to / walk around Amsterdam and with a little organization you can / cover the principal sights within a few days. For the / art lover there is a feast of priceless old masters / to be seen and many collections of modern works. Opera, / ballet and concert enthusiasts are well catered for with a / full theatre season spread throughout the year.

Food ranges from / the traditional Dutch fare, with emphasis on steak, veal, cheese / and egg dishes, to the fascinating spicy delicacies of Indonesian / origin and not unlike Chinese food. This strange influence on / the culinary habits of Holland dates back to the earlier / colonial days of the Dutch East Indies. The sweet tooth / can be satisfied by delicious cream cakes and a variety / of world famous chocolates. (534)

CHAPTER 7
Consonant strokes R and L

Phrasing Drill

Dear John and Barbara, We are writing in this rather / formal way to try to clarify details for the reception. / There are so many suggestions which have been made without / any decisions being taken.

Please let us have your views / about the wedding reception in general terms. We would like / to keep it very informal with speeches to the minimum. / There no longer seems to be any reason for more / than one toast and that is to the bride and / groom. We were all at the Robson reception and we / thought something like that would be ideal. There are so / many things to discuss that it is not possible to / include them all in this letter. If you are able / to get away for an hour or two, perhaps we / could meet next week for lunch and could possibly finalize / matters.

In the meantime, will you please let us know / how many people you will be inviting to the reception, / because we would like to go ahead and make some / arrangements with the hotel of our choice. If we wait / any longer, they will be fully booked for this year / and will be unable to let us have the reception / there. Sincerely, (**202**)

Correspondence

Letter to: Mrs M. Snowdon, Manageress, Pegasus Hotel,

Dear Mrs Snowdon, I would like to confirm the provisional / booking for a wedding reception which I made by telephone / some two weeks' ago. The list is not yet final, / but there will be no less than 80 and no / more than 90 guests.

I would like to think that / the weather will be good enough to consider having the / reception in the hotel gardens as you suggested, but perhaps / we should be realistic and settle for the large lounge. /

There are a number of points to be discussed before / the wedding date, in particular, menus, wine list and floral / decorations. Would you please let us have copies of sample / menus and wine lists so that we can consider them / for a few days before making a decision. After this / I think we should have a meeting. Please let me / know a suitable time for us to have such a / discussion. Almost any morning next week would be very convenient / for me. Yours sincerely, (**164**)

Shorthand Examinations

There are many different examining bodies who set shorthand examinations / and, as you are almost certain to be taking one / of these in the near future, let us have a / look at the variations. The main difference is in the / duration of the dictation. Sometimes it is one passage lasting / for five minutes, or two pieces of four minutes each, / depending on the speed. Another examining body informs candidates that / the dictation time will total eight minutes and will consist / of no less than two or three passages with an / interval between each one.

Past examination papers are for sale / and as far as style of presentation is concerned they / are bound to be something like the dictation you will / have. It is advisable therefore to work through a number / of such papers to familiarize yourself with the examination pattern. / It is important to know well in advance how long / you will have to write, and approximately how many pieces / will be involved. It is very much to our advantage / as shorthand writers to prepare ourselves on the kind of / material that will be used in the examination. Anything like / the same sort of material will be very useful practice / dictation. Are you aware that the '2000' magazine each / month presents no less than four pages of examination passages? /

If you are entering for an examination this year a / decision will have to be made fairly soon about the / speed you should take. This is a difficult decision to / make because it always involves forecasting what your performance will / be quite some time ahead. Your examination speed at any / time is your sustained average writing speed and not a / speed you once achieved for just a minute. If you / are to take an examination at 100 words per minute / you must, by the time of the examination, be / able to write at 100 words per minute for / an extended period and certainly for as long a time / as the total of the examination dictation. As well as / being able to do this you must be able to / write for at least one minute at / 120 words per minute to give yourself a speed reserve. / If you suspect your speed will be any less than / 100 words per minute then you must enter for / a speed lower than 100 words per minute. A / shorthand examination is unique because you cannot do anything like / cramming at the last minute by way of preparation. It / is a matter of a steady build-up of skill. /

Short forms and phrases might well be called the key / to examination success. When all these outlines can be written / at speed, without so much as a fraction of a / second's hesitancy, you will develop real speed potential. Outlines must / be written with accuracy, paying special attention to the size / of strokes, position and the placement of essential vowels.

I / make no apology for repeating the advice given in earlier / chapters of this book that you can help in the / development of writing speed by increasing your speed in the / reading of printed shorthand from the textbook and '2000' / magazine. No longer should you read just for pleasure, but / you should force yourself to read the shorthand as quickly / as possible. Repeat the reading several times and aim to / increase your reading speed at each repetition. There are positive / links between your reading and writing speeds. The faster you / can read shorthand the faster you can write it. Can / you afford to wait any longer before you begin speed / reading? (**601**)

CHAPTER 8
R hook

Phrasing Drill

It appears that there are very few unemployed secretaries and / by far
the larger number of people in this situation / are there because they
do not wish to be employed / at the moment or because they are
living in an / area where jobs are scarce. It does not mean, however, /
that this will always be so and it is in / our interests to qualify ourselves
and be ready for the / day when those without qualifications will have
difficulty in finding / a post. Good qualifications in our own field of
work / help us in our prospects for promotion. Having reached a /
certain speed in shorthand, it is not very far to / the next rung on the
speed ladder and it is / to our advantage to achieve as high a speed
as / possible before leaving a course. This calls for extra effort / and
concentration, but it appears that this is lacking in / some students.

(152)

Correspondence

A circular letter:

Dear Customer, We are having a special sale next month / to clear
goods in all parts of the store for / stocktaking. In our view such a sale
helps us as / much as it can help you, and therefore the price / reductions are quite remarkable. So far this year, as you / are no doubt
aware, we have not entered into any / kind of 'price war' although
many companies throughout the city / seem to advertise cut prices at
frequent intervals. Next month's / sale will, in fact, be the only time

we are / making any special offers and you may be assured that / the bargains will be outstanding and genuine.

As you are / one of our regular and valued customers we are inviting / you to come along at the end of this month, / that is in two weeks' time, to inspect the sale / goods before the sale opens to the general public. You / may take advantage of any of the special offers during / your visit, with the exception of items on display in / the windows which cannot be removed until the official sale / begins. In our own view, by far the most attractive / items are to be found in our jewellery department.

I / look forward to welcoming you to our store once again / in the near future. Yours sincerely, (**216**)

Secretarial Duties

Shorthand-typists and secretaries everywhere spend a considerable amount of / time using their shorthand and typewriting skills, but let us / consider the other functions they carry out during a typical / office day.

One of the most regular tasks is answering / and making telephone calls, and it appears that this is / something which is done noticeably well or somewhat inadequately. When / using a telephone it is important to speak directly into / the mouthpiece and to speak clearly. When answering the telephone / remember to announce the name of your company, or the / telephone number, and this should be followed by a greeting / such as 'Good morning' or 'Good afternoon, Miss Jones speaking, / can I help you?' Always have a notebook or a / message pad beside the telephone with a pen or pencil, / to make notes of any instructions or messages. For my / part, I have always found it is much better to / write whilst the conversation is taking place instead of having / to recall what was said afterwards. Such notes should, of / course, be taken in shorthand. Politeness is essential together with / a business-like attitude but at the same time the / person to whom you are talking should be aware of / a spirit of friendliness and helpfulness. It will be of / considerable assistance to you in improving your telephone technique if / you read the instructions and information contained in the first / few pages of your local telephone directory.

Filing is a / fundamental office routine and by far the most important point / to remember is that this should be done daily. Documents / which are correctly filed are easy to retrieve whenever required, / but an unsorted pile of papers on a desk or / in a basket are of little use to anyone at / any time. There are many different kinds of filing systems / and before entering office life you should be familiar with / the most common and frequently used ones. A textbook on /

office practice will explain the important filing rules and as / long as you observe these you will be successful in / this work.

Reception duties bring the office worker into direct / contact with the public. Always remember that you are seen / by the caller and therefore you must always be looking / at your best, otherwise your approach in dealing with members / of the public should be the same as when talking / to them on the telephone and that is polite, business-like / and friendly. It is up to you to take part / in the efforts made by everyone in your firm to / create an atmosphere that will encourage successful trading. A welcoming / smile from you might put the customer in the right / frame of mind to sign that all-important contract with / your employer. Those born with an outgoing nature will have / few problems, but others will have to work hard at / projecting the right image to the customer and to the / potential customer. 'Tact' and 'diplomacy' should be the key words / throughout the day.

You will also be attending to the / incoming and outgoing mail, making appointments, typing itineraries, and no / doubt ensuring that cups of tea and coffee are available / at the right moment. It may well be your responsibility / to order office stationery, look after the petty cash and / arrange for machine maintenance. If it appears that office life / is just a matter of routine do not be surprised / to find that such a routine is full of interest / and variety. A successful company is a highly complex organisation / and your part is just as important in its way / as that played by the Chief Executive. (597)

CHAPTER 9
L hook

Phrasing Drill

By all accounts, the search for oil continues in what / used to be considered unlikely places. For all countries an / oil discovery is a dream but one which will only / be coming true for a few. It is only comparatively / recently that oil exploration has become so much of a / news item. Some governments have decided that, at all costs, / they must locate any oil deposits which might be within / their boundaries and huge sums of money are being invested / in such searches. By all means in their power oil / companies are examining every possible source in the hope of / making new finds. By all reports, for every new well / successfully sunk there are innumerable disappointments. For all those involved / in this industry, working life, at all times, is a / race against the clock. When millions of pounds are being / spent, it is only too easy to see that every / minute of delay is costing a great deal of money. / (**160**)

Correspondence

Letter to: Mrs G. Lee,

Dear Madam, I have only just been given your name / and address today, although I understand you asked for details / about costs for house decorating last week. I apologize for / the delay caused by a breakdown of communication between the / staff taking annual holidays and those returning from leave.

The / usual practice is for a member of our firm to / visit the home so that an accurate estimate can be / given to the customer. This company specializes in both exterior / and interior decorating and all our work is guaranteed. It / may only take a week to complete the painting of / your house.

By all means come in and discuss our / home improvement loan scheme if you would prefer to spread / the cost over a period of time. Although you have / not been a customer before, it is only a matter / of obtaining one reference, and any necessary work can be / started immediately.

Please write or telephone and let me know / when it will be convenient for someone to call and / give you an estimate. Then, if you wish to discuss / the matter further, I shall be pleased to make the / necessary arrangements. Yours faithfully, Manager (**195**)

Shorthand Speed Development

Shorthand speed does not just happen, but it has to / be worked at in an organized manner. When drilling outlines, / in class or as a homework assignment, you must at / all times say the words to yourself as you write / the outlines. This is your own personal dictation service and / it is far better than simply writing outlines without any / real concentrated effort being involved. My opinion is that you / should always have the key to any exercise you are / practising and in fact, most textbooks today incorporate a key. / This enables you to check any outlines which puzzle you / and, just as important, it makes it possible for a / friend or member of the family to read any exercise / to you. This additional dictation outside the classroom is invaluable, / and it will go a long way to helping you / with your speed development.

Anyone with a tape recorder at / home should use it to full advantage. It is only / just a matter of dictating the passage you have prepared, / counting out the words from the longhand key, and checking / your rate of reading by your wristwatch. After one or / two trial runs at dictating, it is surprising how easy / it is to read at a fairly even speed. This / sort of practice between lessons makes all the difference to / your progress.

If you have access to a language laboratory / or a shorthand laboratory you should make maximum use of / the facilities. Students are advised to read and drill the / practice material, and then tune into one of the four / channels to receive dictation at the speed appropriate to their / individual needs. When timetabled in a shorthand laboratory you must / put some really concentrated effort into the work you will / do there.

Speed reading of shorthand from your textbooks and / '2000' magazine is an excellent method of developing your / rate of writing. The two skills are closely correlated; the / faster you can read shorthand the faster you will write / it. It pays you, therefore, to devote some time each / day to this reading practice. Take any passage of printed / shorthand and read it through as fast as you can. / Encircle any outlines which cause you to hesitate and make / a note of the number of minutes and seconds it / takes you to read the passage. Ask your teacher to / assist you with any outline you cannot read from / '2000' magazine or check the outline from the key if / you are working from one of the textbooks. Drill the / outlines which you could not read and those which caused / you some hesitancy until you know them thoroughly, then repeat / the reading and once again check the time it takes. / Each reading should be faster than the previous one, and / after two or three readings you should be able to / read the material just as quickly as if it was / typewritten. This exercise alone will greatly improve your speed and / it will only take a little of your time, but / to obtain the maximum benefit you should follow through by / taking the same material from dictation. You will now find / it possible to write this well-practised and totally familiar / material at 10 or 20 words per minute above your / ordinary speed, and this increased speed will quickly become an / established part of your skill. (555)

CHAPTER 10
Double-length strokes

Phrasing Drill

In order that you may derive the maximum benefit from / studying this subject, you must give it priority when allocating / time. Some other activities can be left without any harm, / but the skills demand more than their fair share. That / is why many colleges in their planning for skills courses / allow plenty of time for languages, shorthand and typewriting. I / believe there is every justification for this, and I think / there is no need to defend such a policy.

Secretarial / students have to depend upon their skills to earn their / living, and the majority see the necessity for devoting sufficient / time each day to practice. If there is to be / any progress there has to be practice and preparation. When / there is not enough time some other ways or some / other means will have to be found, for there is / no substitute for reading printed shorthand. So find that extra / time by reading on the bus or train. Some students / even read 2000 in their baths! (**167**)

Correspondence

Letter to: Mr David Winter, Manager, Central Motors Limited,

Dear Sir, Several friends have recommended that I write to / you to make arrangements about car hire because, in their / opinion, your company offers the very best service and terms. / I depend upon their judgement in such matters because they / have travelled extensively throughout Europe, and this trip will be / my first.

I will be arriving in England in the / middle of June and I will need a motor-car / for one month. Let me say straight away that I / do not want anything which is very dear, but a / simple vehicle which is capable of transporting two adults and / one child. I know there is not such a wide / range in the smaller cars, but I must stress that / the economics of the whole trip are based on being / able to obtain a car at a reasonable rental.

As / soon as I have full information from you about the / current rates, and I have decided that they are satisfactory, / I shall send you a deposit in order that I / can be assured of a vehicle being reserved for me. / Yours faithfully, (**182**)

Theatre

How long is it since you have been to a / theatre and experienced that very special magic of live entertainment? / There can be an almost electric atmosphere during any show, / with a unique form of communication between the actors and / the audience. Whilst the main action is coming from the / stage there is a distinct and a measurable response or / feedback from the public. Out of their enthusiasm is born / the added dimension which is totally lacking in any other / form of entertainment.

In recent times many theatres have closed, / and this has in most cases been the direct result / of competition from motion pictures and television. The arrival of / silent films in the early part of this century was / the first blow and this was quickly followed and intensified / when 'the talkies' arrived. When the Hollywood film industry captured / and entertained millions of people throughout the world, the live / theatre did manage to survive. The advent of television saw / the closure of more theatres and even rocked the very / foundations of the film-making industry. At one time no / town centre was complete without its music hall or variety / theatre. Most of these have vanished, making way for some / other form of entertainment such as discos or bingo, or / remaining shuttered and boarded-up until the arrival of the / property developer.

In spite of these traumatic events the public / still flocked to see the large scale musical shows, many / of which had long and successful runs. A good play / could still draw an appreciative audience. All world records have / been broken by one play in London called 'The Mousetrap', / which has been running for more than twenty years. The / long established British pantomime has continued to attract large crowds / particularly family groups, commencing before Christmas each year and then / extending until well into the winter. I believe there is / no better outing for the whole family than a visit / to the pantomime.

Let there be no doubt, however, the / theatre is still struggling for its very existence. Ever rising / costs of production make it almost impossible to recover expenses, / let alone leave a profit for the people who have / invested their money in the venture. Even with government support / in the form of national grants and financial assistance from / local authorities there is still a constant battle to remain / solvent. What is needed to keep our theatres open? The / most important thing is public support. If you merely sympathize / with those who support this work but do not attend / regularly yourself, then your local centre for the performing arts / might well close. Once closed there is little hope of / its ever opening again.

The most enthusiastic supporters are the / various amateur societies who not only put on their own / shows but go along and see all the other amateur / productions in their area. Frequently these shows are as good / as, or even better than, their professional counterparts.

Many areas / have a local repertory company which puts on a season / of plays and sometimes musical entertainments throughout the year in / their own theatre. This is a professional company which is / able to support itself from the money you pay at / the box office. I think there is no doubt that / in order that such a theatre shall continue its work / it must have regular visits from you, your family and / friends. (561)

CHAPTER 11
Omission of a word

Phrasing Drill

For a time in shorthand speed development nothing seems to / be happening. Your notes appear to get rougher and rougher, / or larger and larger. You are at a loss to / know what to do. But just pause for a minute / and consider the facts of the case. There must have / been a time in the past, in fact only a / few weeks ago, when you had no shorthand skill. Keep / in mind that this is a new achievement, and already / you have made good progress in it side by side / with typewriting.

First and foremost keep your mind on the / target and continually strive to reach it. Now and then / you may feel tempted to give up but this is / out of the question. I am sorry to say that / I have come to the conclusion that some students do / not work hard enough. The fact of the matter is / they think success will arrive automatically. For those who are / really trying their best, will you please remember that success / takes time. There have been, and are, students throughout the / world who feel for a time that progress is too / slow, but in a way this is to be expected. / One fact is certain, with continued hard work, speed does / develop. **(211)**

Correspondence

Dear Pat, Sorry not to have written for a long / time, but you know me, full of promises! Anyway, it / has not been entirely my fault. The fact of the / matter is that I have been so busy at College / and there seems to have been no time left for / correspondence. The holidays are almost here and that is what / I am writing to you about. Can I take up / your offer to visit you at the end of this / month? Will you please reply as soon as possible and / let me know? I appreciate that with so little notice / it might not be possible.

While I am visiting you / perhaps we can go to a concert by one of / the many groups which seem to appear so frequently at / your City Hall, or do you think getting tickets will / be out of the question at this stage? Not that / I am suggesting you wait all night for tickets— no / group is worth that sacrifice! Do try to see if / any are available, but also bear in mind that funds / are low. I have come to the conclusion that my / income cannot stretch to all the luxuries I enjoy! Sincerely, / (**200**)

Transcription

There must have been a great deal said about the / art of transcription, and it all must have been said / again and again—yet problems do still exist. I have / come to the conclusion that the main issue is the / inability of the writer to read what has been written. / The reason, I am sorry to say, is a lack / of precision in the position writing of outlines and the / placement of essential vowels. All shorthand writers must keep in / mind that shorthand is only written to be transcribed. Notes / are not left for a long time in the notebook / but are put into a typewritten form quite quickly after / the dictation. First and foremost writers must aim for and / achieve total accuracy in their notes. A careless, inaccurate note / is out of the question. Now and then a note / may become slightly less than perfect when the dictation is / very rapid, often resulting in the outlines becoming larger and / larger and rougher and rougher, but even then, accuracy of / position can and must be maintained. That is why it / is important to acquire a writing speed as high as / 140 words a minute even if it / is only for a minute. Such a speed will enable / you to cope with almost any dictation and as a / result you will feel confident and your notes will become / better and better.

In addition to the notes, transcription can / be helped by the correct usage of the notebook. Always / have a margin on each page. In the classroom this / is used by the teacher to draw your attention to / the number of errors made. In offices throughout the world / writers use the margin to insert a query sign against / a line of shorthand in which there is a point / to be cleared at the conclusion of the dictation. Any / problem in relation to the dictated matter can be resolved / without any loss of time or interruption.

I am at / a loss to understand the argument for writing longhand in / shorthand notes with one exception, and that is never to / write anything but shorthand except when you are given a / spelling. As a rule, the dictator will only do this / in the event of there being an alternative and for / the sake of transcription ease you must write out the / spelling in longhand.

Year by year, students encounter problems in / connection with punctuation. The fact of the matter is that / a punctuation sign is just as important as an outline / and must be written into the note side by side / with the outlines. When you 'hear' a full stop, or / the beginning of a new paragraph, will you please punctuate / your notes accordingly. Shorthand is not a memory aid and / your notes should be capable of being read at the / present time even though they were written a week, a / month or, on the very rare occasion, a year ago. /

As quickly as possible in your training, that is to / say immediately you have a typewriting speed of over 20 / words a minute, you should begin typewriting from shorthand outlines. / In the first place, you should return to a very / early exercise in your shorthand textbook, read it through again / several times, and then type it. After some practice on / such material you can move on to shorthand notes you / have written as fair copy work, and the final step / is to type from notes taken in dictation. This is / what your training has been all about. (**587**)

CHAPTER 12
N hook

Phrasing Drill

I have been using a pen for shorthand notes for / longer than I care to remember, and I believe in / my own case this is the very best writing instrument. / Most people can achieve a good writing style with a / pen because it is much better than a pencil. A / student using a pencil sharpens it in class and starts / writing, but she has been writing for only a very / short time before the point becomes blunt or breaks and / she has to re-sharpen it again; this goes on throughout / the lesson.

For your own good, as you develop your / shorthand skill take time and care when choosing your writing / instrument. No one else can successfully do this for you; / it must be your own selection. Anything selected by somebody / else might be larger than, or smaller than is suitable / for you. We all have our own preferences. Before purchasing / the pen, it is also wise to write shorthand with / it in the shop, rather than waiting until you get / home and finding it is not suitable, or it is / faulty. (**181**)

Correspondence

Letter to : Mrs Frances Adams,

Dear Mrs Adams, I have been meaning to write to / you for a long time to tell you that I / am still continuing with my shorthand studies. After leaving college, / I took your advice and enrolled at an evening class / for speed development. I now have a certificate for / 120 words a minute which, after the slow / start I made in the subject, is better than I / expected.

Having become so interested in shorthand, I now want / more than anything else to become a high speed writer / and if it is possible to work in the Law / Courts. I realize, of course, that my speed will have / to be greater than it is now. From your own / experience can you tell me what target I should be / setting myself? Can you also advise me what steps to / take to get into this type of work? I am / very keen to travel the world and I think this / would be possible if I qualify as a court reporter. / I look forward to hearing from you. Yours sincerely, (**179**)

Working Abroad

No longer is it possible for anyone from anywhere to / pack up their bags and go to live and work / in some other part of the world. The age of / colour television, flights to the moon and similar technological advances / has also produced an immense amount of paper work, rules / and regulations, which prevent or certainly impede migration.

Visiting different / countries throughout the world on holiday presents few problems, usually / no more than the necessity for a current passport, sometimes / a visa or a valid smallpox certificate, and the possession / of a return ticket. During such visits the seeking of / any form of employment is usually prohibited.

Anyone wishing to / leave their own country to work permanently or temporarily in / another country must go through a complex, and often time- / consuming routine to clear all formalities. Governments in most countries / demand that an immigrant shall possess skills and qualifications which / are needed at that particular time, with a guarantee of / employment on arrival, a good state of health, and with / sufficient cash to keep him or her financially independent until / they are earning money. Sometimes there is even a further / restriction of a specified number of immigrants being allowed into / a country during any one year and once that quota / has been completed no further applications will be considered.

So / how does one go about getting a post abroad and / fulfilling all the requirements of the government concerned? First of / all, the better your basic qualifications are the easier it / will be to persuade the authorities that you are a / desirable applicant. Specialist qualifications do help. By reading the national / newspapers of the countries in which you are interested it / is possible to obtain an idea of the qualifications which / employers will expect. Such overseas papers can be read at / many of our public libraries or can be purchased at / one of the larger newsagents. A great deal of information / is available at the embassy or consular offices for personal / callers or in answer to written enquiries.

Advertisements for posts / abroad regularly appear in our own national papers and the / companies or organizations seeking staff smooth the way through the / red tape involved. International companies are used to transferring staff / around the world and to recruiting new employees for their / many offices and factories, and the would-be immigrant has / fewer problems when applying through one of these international employers. /

Before accepting any post in another country, it is wise / to check, if possible with an impartial third party who / has recently been there, that the salary being offered is / as good as it seems. The cost of living in / our own country may appear high but it could be / a great deal higher elsewhere. What seems to be a / very attractive high salary at interview might, in fact, be / totally inadequate for the part of the world in which / it will be necessary to work.

Armed with a good / general education, and having successfully completed a secretarial course, the / world is indeed your oyster—that is the English-speaking / world. For those who wish to work in a country / where English is not the mother tongue it will be / useful, if not essential, to have at least a working / knowledge of the language of that country. (547)

CHAPTER 13
F and V hook

Phrasing Drill

The rates of interest charged by banks and building societies / vary a great deal but it is the state of / the country's economy at any one time which has the / greatest influence. Those who have been involved in borrowing money / for any purpose will have been charged a certain rate / of interest. We would be better off saving for smaller / items, such as a car, and paying cash at the / time of purchase.

Almost everyone, however, will have to make / arrangements for a home loan, and when paying all that / interest there is the consolation that the government may offset / part of the sum you have to pay as interest / against your income tax. In spite of the many promises / by the various political parties, interest rates remain high. Instead / of being cut, these rates are often increased quite deliberately / in support of a move to reduce public spending. Such / events create resentment. A new set of financial rules are / needed to get the country out of its many financial / problems. (**171**)

Correspondence

Letter to: Miss J. Job, Editor, '2000' Magazine, 41 Parker Street, London WC2B 5PB, England.

Dear Miss Job, I have been taking '2000' magazine / now for almost a year, and I am writing to / tell you how very useful it has been throughout my / secretarial course. In fact it has really been a part / of the course, because we have used it extensively in / shorthand, typewriting and office practice classes. We have been encouraged / to read every shorthand outline which appeared in each issue, / and after it has been read most of the material / is drilled and written from dictation.

I have enjoyed many / of the articles which have appeared on the subject of / careers. You are to be congratulated on the wide range / of topics and the variety of reading material. Even though / I am completing my course at college this term I / will be continuing with my regular order for a copy / of '2000', and you will have heard that a / number of my friends will be doing likewise. I think / it will be of great benefit to me during my / first months of working life, and I shall have plenty / of time to read it during my journey to and / from the office each day.

At all events we shall / be better off if we continue with our shorthand speed / classes until we all have certificates for at least / 120 words per minute and '2000' will / help us to achieve our ambitions. Yours sincerely, (**238**)

Gardening

Gardening can be a joy or a chore, a pleasure / or sheer hard work. Your own attitude will normally depend / upon how you were introduced to gardening. For a great / number of people it is a wonderful relaxation, and an / activity which takes the mind off the troubles of the / day. It provides plenty of exercise for those who worry / about their own lack of activity, and the demands of / gardening are such that no one can be lazy and / get away with it.

There is considerable joy in planting / very ordinary-looking things like seeds and bulbs and seeing / them grow into beautiful plants and flowers. For the family / moving into a newly-built house, there is a tremendous / challenge in the planning and development of a new garden / and plenty of hard but rewarding work ahead.

Years ago / a vegetable garden was sometimes included by families keen to / have fresh produce, but it was usually hidden away in / a corner. Today there is a much greater emphasis on / growing vegetables because of the high cost of all food. / A family can be almost self-supporting in vegetables with / quite a small garden, a tiny financial investment, and two / or three hours a week labour. A household which has / a deep-freeze unit can make even greater use of / the garden harvest by freezing the surplus crops.

For the / millions of people who have no garden, all is not / lost, because you have many opportunities open to you to / bring flowers and the growing of plants into your life. / Indoor gardening is one of the fastest-growing hobbies in / the world. House plants are to be found in large / homes and tiny bed-sitters. In return for a little / time and loving care, plants bloom and give a profusion / of flowers week after week. Even during the resting period / the greenery of the foliage can make a pleasing display / in any room of the home. A wide range of / tropical plants may be seen in the dining rooms and / living rooms of houses in even the coldest climates as / a result of the modern methods of central heating.

How / refreshing it is to see a splash of living colour / in many offices today, sometimes planted by the person responsible / for the interior decoration or just because someone brought a / plant into work and it thrived. The watering and feeding / of office plants is frequently a part of the office / junior's duties. In large organizations it is possible that a / full-time gardener is employed to attend to window-boxes / and the large variety of plants scattered throughout the multi- / storey office block.

One of the most gardening-conscious countries / in the world is Holland. The growing of flowers and / bulbs is on a gigantic commercial scale and is a / very important part of the Dutch economy. But the Dutch / people love flowers too, and have filled their homes and / gardens with beautiful floral displays. In the spring-time you / will even see motor-cars swathed in garlands of daffodils. / Houseboats on the canals have flowerpots everywhere and, naturally, the / public parks with their magnificent floral exhibitions attract thousands of / visitors from all parts of the world. (**537**)

CHAPTER 14

Shun hook
Vocalization in phrases
Disjoining in phrases

Phrasing Drill

Young men on both sides of the Atlantic Ocean become / members of
various associations, but very few are qualified to / join the Medical
Association or the Football Association. Many young / men and women
do join the Automobile Association, however, and / most motorists
find it to their benefit to take out / such membership. If you join an
Association, it is most / probable that free advice and assistance will
be available to / you should you require it in the year that is / covered
by your fee. Membership is usually for the year, / but it might be
possible to join on a half- / yearly or quarterly basis. It is not necessary
to worry / about when to pay each time because a reminder is / sent
out. If there is an increase in the fee, / your attention will be drawn to
this in good time. / Associations are by no means limited to those with
professional / qualifications. You will see at least ten or more announce-
ments / in any newspaper from groups of people with common
interests. / (**170**)

Correspondence

Letter to: Doctor B. Taylor,

Dear Dr Taylor, Thank you for your application for membership / of
the Medical Association. I am returning your cheque, however, /
because you will see that you did not sign it. / As soon as I receive the
signed cheque I will / proceed with the application. It might be more
convenient for / you to pay for the fees by bankers order and / I am

enclosing the forms with this letter. It is / not necessary for these to be completed immediately but if / you are planning to use this method of paying, I / should receive them at least three months before the next / payment is due.

Please contact me if there is any / other way in which the Association can be of assistance / to you. When I send your membership card, I will / also let you have a copy of the Medical Association / handbook for the year just beginning. We are not able / to issue this publication to people who are not members / of the Medical Association. Yours sincerely, Secretary (**167**)

Special Occasion

For many people there is only one way to celebrate / an anniversary or birthday, and that is by going out / for a meal to a restaurant or hotel. All too / often these events are disappointing for a variety of reasons, / but it seems probable that the cause may have been / lack of planning on the part of the host. Any / establishment which has a deservedly good reputation will be fully / booked well in advance for a Friday or Saturday evening / and, therefore, it is important to make a reservation at / least several days ahead of the date you require. The / danger is that if it is not possible to get / into the restaurant of your first choice it might be / decided to settle for another just to celebrate that particular / date, and the second choice may not be satisfactory.

Ask / around amongst friends and colleagues for the names of places / they can really recommend for there is nothing better than / a personal recommendation. Newspaper articles about excellent eating places are / frequently sponsored by the restaurants themselves and the owners pay / for the space the paper devotes to these articles. There / are, of course, some very reliable book guides which appear / annually and these usually give a fair and unbiased point / of view, for those who need it.

In any case, / if the meal is to be followed by a visit / to the theatre, or a meeting with friends, it is / very important to allow sufficient time to eat in comfort. / There is nothing worse than watching the clock and having / to rush a meal. It might be better to have / the meal after the show, provided it is not necessary / to hurry because it is getting near to closing time / and the waiter seems to be throwing the food at / you! To be enjoyable a meal must have plenty of / time allocated to it. If an emergency overtakes you and / time is precious, then restrict yourself to a main course / and coffee. This will save time, prevent loss of temper, / avoid indigestion, and in no way spoil the celebration.

When / making a restaurant reservation it is wise to ask about / any dressing formalities. Holiday resort hotels are usually quite relaxed / about how people dress for lunch, but often insist upon / something a little more formal for dinner, the ladies wearing / a dress and the gentlemen a suit and tie. There / is nothing more embarrassing than arriving for a meal only / to be turned away because one of the party is / not correctly dressed. The most common fault is for one / of the men not to be wearing a tie. Some / enterprising managers have a spare tie available for those who / arrive without one.

I know that some waiters occasionally try / to take advantage of the host by endeavouring to force / expensive dishes or highly-priced bottles of wine upon him, / knowing that in company many people will go beyond their / planned budget rather than appear mean. One must remember that / this is by no means always the case, indeed it / may happen only once in the year. So, if you / are a guest, take the lead from your host, and / go to his or her rescue when under attack by / suggesting some alternative and cheaper items on the menu. It / might clear the way for the host to make the / final decision without being brow-beaten by the waiter. (569)

CHAPTER 15
Disjoining for CON, COM

Phrasing Drill

After his return from holiday remind Mr Jones about the / next committee meeting which is due to take place on / Friday. There is a vacancy and there will have to / be an election. He will be involved on committee work / for at least a day. The committee is anxious to / clear up all outstanding points before the end of the / year. With his very considerable number of commitments during the / next month, suggest that he does not accept any more / engagements. He must make arrangements to see the accountant in / connection with income tax returns for this year.

It is / urgent that he talks to John London of International Electronics / who is complaining about unfair competition, and claims he is / entitled to the protection set out in the contract. The / editor of the 'Evening Chronicle' would like to discuss an / article on the firm which is to appear in a / special Business Feature Section next week.

Also remind him about / the interviews for next week in connection with the appointment / of someone to be in control of export orders. (**179**)

Correspondence

Memo to Terence Sparrow, Personnel Department, from General Manager, subject: RECRUITMENT, today's date:

Please make arrangements to visit the local College of Further / Education to interview the girls who are about to complete / a course of secretarial training. You will recall that our / visit was very successful last year and we were able / to offer posts to a number of students. If you / contact the Head of Business Studies as soon as possible / you should be able to agree on a time suitable / for all concerned.

Although it is still early in the / calendar year, it is not long before the students commence / a heavy programme of examination commitments, and shortly after that / they seem to obtain positions very quickly and are not / interested in coming for an interview. Perhaps you might consider / the idea of taking Marion along with you. It is / now two years since she joined the organization from a / course at the college and she will be able to / give a different point of view. The company is anxious / to establish closer contact with all colleges in the area, / and although it appears at this time that we shall / be unable to consider as many applicants for jobs as / last year, our offices in other parts of the country / may be able to take any really good candidates and / offer them accommodation in our hostels. **(216)**

The Skill of Shorthand Writing

Now that you are about to complete this book you / should be feeling very confident about your ability to write / shorthand. You have a sound knowledge of all the phrasing / principles and after some concentrated practice using these phrasing devices, / you will be able to write at speeds up to / 150 words per minute. This is assuming / that you are already totally familiar with the short forms / and intersections which you learned while studying 'First Course'.

It / must be stressed that speed cannot develop unless you do / know and can recall and write every short form and / intersection instantly and with confidence. This confidence must be extended / to all the phrases you have encountered in *Skill Book*. / Armed with this knowledge there is absolutely no reason why / you should not make steady progress up the speed ladder. / For the really high speed enthusiast there is a further / course of study available to take him or her beyond / the 150 words per minute speed level. / This is only necessary for the person who is interested / in taking up verbatim work in the Courts or who / is simply wanting to write at speeds above those required / by the average employer.

To all writers of Pitman 2000 / I wish to say a few words about the / skill you are now able to use. The system you / have learned is very precise and it will be found / that it can stand up to the strain of any / dictation in today's business world. The system is good, but / only as good as the person using it. At all / times you must be an accurate writer, who is in / control of outlines and writing them accurately in their correct / first, second or third positions. When you write a half-/length stroke, make sure that it is written half the / length of a normal stroke, and when writing a double-/length stroke always write it double the length of a / normal stroke. When you glance at your notes there should / never be any doubt as to whether or not a / stroke is ordinary, half- or double-length. There must be / a very considerable difference in the size of such strokes. /

At this stage of learning you should be familiar with / all the vowel signs and know where to place them / in each outline. When you are confident about the placing / of these signs it is possible and highly desirable for / you to leave many of them out. The result is / that you will vocalize only certain outlines which could be / difficult to read without the placing of an essential vowel / sign, and usually it is not necessary to place more / than one sign to any outline. Remember that short outlines / with perhaps only one consonant stroke or a half-length / stroke must have a vowel sign, and a good general / rule is always to place a diphthong sign. An outline / which has a diphone should be examined and if you / feel you would have difficulty in reading it without the / sign, for example the word 'area', then you should always / add the sign whenever you write such an outline.

Your / employer will pay you to produce a well-typed and / accurate transcript so take care with your spelling. (**548**)